Property of
LAINGSBURG COMMUNITY
MIDDLE SCHOOL LIBRARY

D1238763

WINSTON CHURCHILL
Lion of Britain

The Yin and the Yang, *an ancient Chinese figure, is symbolic for Century Books, since both negative and positive forces which the figure represents also shape the lives of famous world figures.*

According to folklore, the Yin and the Yang are present in all things, functioning together in perpetual interaction. This balance between opposing forces, and the influences, both good and bad, that have molded the course of history are accurately portrayed as background material in Century biographies.

WINSTON CHURCHILL
Lion of Britain

by Sam and Beryl Epstein

A CENTURY BOOK

GARRARD PUBLISHING COMPANY
CHAMPAIGN, ILLINOIS

Picture credits:

Bettmann Archive: p. 69
Brown Brothers: p. 40
Central Press Photos Ltd—Pictorial Parade: pp. 98, 113
Toni Frissell: p. 163
Karsh, Ottawa: p. 136
London Daily Express—Pictorial Parade: pp. 41, 62
Paris Match—Pictorial Parade: pp. 104, 153
Photoworld: pp. 79, 160
Radio Times Hulton Picture Library: pp. 11, 16 (both), 30, 50
United Press International: pp. 27, 118, 127 (both), 133, 150, jacket
Wide World Photos: pp. 19, 144, 157

Copyright © 1971 by Sam and Beryl Epstein
All rights reserved. Manufactured in the U.S.A.
Standard Book Number: 8116–4752–8
Library of Congress Catalog Card Number: 78–146704

Contents

1. Lord Randolph's Son

Winston Churchill, Royal Military College cadet, put the gold watch his father had given him into his breast pocket before setting out for a walk one chilly spring Sunday in 1894. He was relieved that the watch had come back from the London repair shop that week looking as good as new. Now his father need never know that it had been badly damaged when another cadet bumped into him and sent it crashing to the ground.

Lord Randolph, Winston felt sure, would have called that accident an example of criminal negligence on his son's part. He would have expressed his opinion with that icy glare that intimidated even his colleagues in Parliament.

At the bank of a little stream that ran through the college grounds Winston bent down to pick up a stick. The watch fell out of his pocket into the water.

For a moment he could only stare at the spot where it had fallen. Everywhere else the stream was shallow. Everywhere else its bottom was visible beneath a scant few inches of water. Only at this spot, where the watch had disappeared, was there a pool at least six feet deep.

He stripped off his uniform and dove into the pool.

Frantically he searched among the weeds and stones on the bottom, feeling for the little leather pouch he had had made to protect his father's gift. When he had to come up for air, he waited only long enough to suck in one deep breath before he went down again.

The water was so icy that his fingers soon became numb. At the end of ten agonizing minutes he had to give up.

Early the next morning Winston was in the office of the governor of the school, asking permission to have the pool dredged. The permission was granted and the operation took place the same day. It proved useless. The watch could not be found.

Tuesday morning he was again in the governor's office, this time with a more elaborate request. The governor hesitated.

"Don't worry, sir," Winston assured him. "Everything will look just at it does now when I have finished."

He sounded very confident. He left with the permission he sought.

Minutes later he had rounded up twenty-three men from the infantry unit attached to the school.

"I'll pay you fair wages," he told them, "for making a new course for this stream. Please detour the stream around the deep pool."

"How do we go about making a course?" somebody queried.

"You dig it," Winston explained. "Just as you dig a battlefield trench."

They understood him then. Everyone at Sandhurst, as the Royal Military College was usually called, had to learn to dig trenches.

"When it's ready," Winston went on, "we'll dam the stream above the pool and let the water flow into its new course." He picked up his own shovel. "Just one more thing," he added. "Remove the top layer of soil carefully so that when we finish we can put everything back just the way it is now."

They dug a ditch-like stream bed and built the dam. They led the stream into its new course. Finally no water remained in the original bed except for that in the six-foot pool.

"Now I'll borrow the fire engine pump and pump that dry," Winston said.

As soon as the pool was empty he climbed into it.

There, at last, half-buried on the bottom, he found his watch. The works were already coated with rust.

"Thus early did Winston reveal his resourcefulness, his ability to organize and his talent for command," Winston's son Randolph wrote many years later in his biography of his father.

Winston would probably have agreed matter-of-factly with those admiring words, but on the day he found his watch and shipped it back to the London repair shop, it was his father's opinion of him that was his greatest concern. Just lately, since he had become a cadet, his father had made a companion of him for the first time. Together they had gone to the theater; they had attended the races when Lord Randolph's horses were running; Lord Randolph had even taken Winston along to a weekend gathering of Conservative party leaders at Lord Rothschild's country home. Winston had begun to let himself believe that when Lord Randolph became prime minister of England—as Winston felt sure he would someday—Winston would be beside him as his trusted aide.

The watch had not yet been returned to him when he received a letter from his father. Lord Randolph was furious. In the London repair shop, on an errand of his own, he had learned of "the shameful way" Winston had treated his gift. Lord Randolph had been told that the watch had been in the shop not long before "badly broken," and that it was there now in a "horribly rusty" state.

"I would not believe you could be such a young stupid," Lord Randolph concluded.

Winston wrote him immediately. His letter was long and he took great pains with it. He told his father about the cadet who had bumped into him and caused the first accident. He told him how much time and money he had spent to retrieve the watch from the pool.

Winston's father, Lord Randolph Spencer-Churchill,
was a prominent member of Parliament.

"Please don't judge me entirely on the strength of the watch," he begged.

Lord Randolph did not immediately send him the forgiveness he hoped for. Winston wrote again. And again.

At last came the words he had so anxiously awaited, in a brief note: "You need not trouble any more about the watch."

In the following weeks, however, there were no further invitations from his father. Instead, suddenly, came the news that Lord Randolph's poor health made it necessary for him and Lady Randolph to take a long trip. They left London almost immediately for a voyage around the world. They were away for six months.

When they returned, Lord Randolph was already close to death. He died a few weeks later, shortly after his son's twentieth birthday.

"Had he lived another four or five years, he could not have done without me," Winston wrote long afterward. "But there were no four or five years!"

Winston's son Randolph viewed the death of his grandfather in another light. In his father's biography he wrote: "There was now no one to help him—or stand in his way; for if Lord Randolph had lived, even in better health, he would have been an obstacle to Winston's career and prospects which were soon to burgeon. He was free to leave the nest . . ."

2. "School Will Discipline Him"

Winston Leonard Spencer-Churchill—the name the family used at that time was Spencer-Churchill—was born November 30, 1874, in the huge palace called Blenheim. It belonged to his grandfather, the seventh duke of Marlborough.

The duke's title, like his home, had come down to him from his eighteenth century ancestor, the first duke of Marlborough, one of England's greatest military heroes. That first duke had chosen as his motto the words "Faithful but Unfortunate," because he felt he had been unfairly treated by his enemies at home while he was fighting his country's French foes abroad. Most people thought him fortunate indeed when a grateful queen honored him with a dukedom and built for him a palace of some 300 rooms.

Set in the vast rolling acres of what had been a royal park, Blenheim was said to be the most magnificent palace in all England. The first duke of Marlborough had named it for the European town where he had won his most famous victory.

Church bells rang out in Woodstock, the village beside the palace, to announce Winston's birth. Those bells always rang when a possible heir to the dukedom was born. If Winston's father's older brother died, and left no heirs, Winston would inherit his grandfather's title and his great estate.

All the traditions of a noble English heritage thus surrounded Winston when he came into the world.

He had another remarkable heritage too. Jennie, Lady Randolph, his beautiful dark-haired mother, was the daughter of the colorful American millionaire Leonard Jerome.

Jerome's Huguenot ancestors had first settled in America in 1710. One of them married a relative of George Washington. Jerome himself married a girl whose grandmother, it was rumored, was an Iroquois Indian. Son of a farmer, and one of ten children, he had worked to help put himself through college. Leonard Jerome had made his first fortune while he was still a young man. When he lost that fortune he made another one just as easily.

Jerome loved to drive his handsome horses at breakneck speed. He took part in the first transatlantic yacht race, helping crew the winning vessel through stormy December seas. He and his friends listened to their favorite opera singers in the private theater he had built beside his New York mansion. He enjoyed buying the fine jewels and clothes his wife and three daughters wore when they joined Europe's fashionable society.

Jennie was his favorite daughter. She had his wit and courage and his unbounded energy. She was nineteen when she wrote him that she wanted to marry twenty-three-year-old Lord Randolph Spencer-Churchill, who had proposed to her three days after they met.

Jerome sent her his delighted consent. He withdrew it angrily when he learned how the duke of Marlborough had reacted to the news.

"This Mr. J. seems to be a sporting, and I should think vulgar kind of man," the duke had written to Randolph. Marrying into the Jerome family, the duke felt, would not be "respectable."

The young people refused to give each other up. Randolph had never expected to have to support himself, but now he began to talk of going off somewhere —anywhere—to earn a living for Jennie and himself.

Then the Conservative member of Parliament for the Blenheim village of Woodstock resigned. The duke himself had filled that seat in the House of Commons before he had inherited his title. He had always wanted his son to follow in his footsteps. He asked Randolph to run for election against the Liberal party's candidate.

Randolph seized the chance.

"All tricks are fair in love and war," he wrote Jennie exultantly.

He had no serious interest in politics as yet. He had agreed to enter the race only because his father had

Jennie Churchill was regarded as one of the most beautiful women in all of England. She gave birth to Winston at Blenheim (below), home of her husband's family and ancestors.

said he would approve their early marriage if Randolph won.

His exuberant campaign was successful. He and Jennie were married soon afterward. A member of the House of Commons received no salary, but the duke was now willing to give his son a generous allowance. The young couple received another allowance from Leonard Jerome. Jennie made their fashionable little London house a popular gathering place for Randolph's titled friends. Both of them were favorites of the Prince of Wales, who was then as merry as his mother, the widowed Queen Victoria, was staid.

To Jennie there was always something chill and forbidding about Blenheim's huge courtyard, its great tapestried state chambers, its endless halls. She was sorry that, as Randolph's wife, she had to visit the place several times during the first year of her marriage. She was at Blenheim when her first child arrived, some weeks before he was expected. The baby was christened Winston, for the father of the first duke of Marlborough, and Leonard for his American grandfather.

The excitement over Winston's birth died quickly. Like most children of well-to-do English families of those days, he was kept out of sight in his nursery. His mother might stop in to see him on her way to dress for dinner. She never had time to stay long.

"She shone for me like the Evening Star," Winston

wrote of her years later. "I loved her dearly—but at a distance."

The only person who played with him, who talked to him and held him on her lap was Mrs. Everest, his nurse. She was plump, warmhearted, and affectionate. With her he went for walks on fine days and played indoors with his toy soldiers when it rained. She went along with him on visits to Blenheim and comforted him when he was scolded by his grandmother, the duchess. When his family spent many months in Ireland, while the duke served as Queen Victoria's viceroy there, Mrs. Everest went to Ireland too and taught Winston to ride a donkey.

His brother Jack, born when Winston was five, was too young to be a playmate for him. He seldom saw his cousins or any other boys or girls of his age. But he was happy with Mrs. Everest.

"Winston, my darling, you are going to have a governess," Mrs. Everest told him one day.

"Why?" Winston demanded.

"Because it is time you had regular lessons, love," she said.

"You are teaching me to read," Winston said. "I don't want any other lessons!"

He ran away and hid the day the governess arrived. Mrs. Everest organized a search party and brought him home.

Even when he was a boy, Winston's bearing expressed his rebellious spirit and his strong character.

He had been sure he wouldn't like the governess. He didn't.

One day he rang for the maid who hurried to the nursery thinking the governess needed her. "Take her away," Winston said imperiously, pointing to the governess. "She is very cross."

If the governess told him to memorize a list of words, he could learn them quickly if he wanted to.

"But I don't see why I have to!" he said. "You can't make me do it!"

"Don't talk back to me, Winston," she warned him, "or I shall have to speak to Lord Randolph about you."

Winston was too young to understand it at the time, but his father was just beginning to talk back himself, to the older men who had long led the ruling Tory, or Conservative party. Tory leaders were startled and angry.

"The only excuse I can find for Randolph," the duke of Marlborough wrote to a friend, "is that he must either be mad or have been singularly affected with local champagne..."

In 1880 the Tories lost the election and their position of power. Lord Randolph, who had kept his own seat in the House of Commons, felt his party leaders had deserved their defeat. In fiery speeches, inside and out of the House of Commons, he began urging people to demand a new kind of Tory party policy which he called Tory Democracy. Soon thousands of workers and farmers, who had never trusted Tory aristocrats, began to accept him as their leader. His act of rebellion had transformed him into one of the most important men in the country.

Lord Randolph was not amused, however, when he learned that his young son seemed to be a rebel. "School will discipline him," he said.

Winston was almost eight years old when his mother took him to St. George's School, some twenty-five miles from London. The other boys took one look at his red hair and called him "Carrots."

Winston didn't mind the nickname. He was proud that his hair was red, like his father's. He did feel frightened and lonely, however, among so many other boys, most of them older than himself. He was determined that no one should know how he felt.

He deliberately broke rules. Boys were not permitted to enter the school pantry, but Winston went in one day and took some sugar. He was caught. "Bring him to my study," the headmaster ordered sternly.

Two of the older boys led Winston to the room where the headmaster was waiting with a thin birch rod in his hand. They halted in front of a box covered with black cloth.

"Take down your trousers," one boy ordered.

"Now kneel in front of the box," the other said. "Put your head on it." Both boys clamped their hands over the red head, pressing it against the box.

The headmaster raised his whip and brought it down.

The pain was worse than anything Winston had ever known. He clenched his teeth. He had made up his mind that he would not cry out no matter how much he was hurt. At each stroke the whip cut into his bared flesh.

"Twenty strokes," the headmaster said finally. "That should be enough to teach him to obey our rules."

"On your feet," one of the older boys said. "Pull up your trousers."

Dozens of other boys had gathered in the hall, as they always did, to listen to the shrieks of a boy who was being beaten. Today they had heard nothing. As Winston left the study, they stared at him with curiosity and amazement.

Winston thrust out his chin and walked past them toward the door. On a rack near the door hung the headmaster's straw hat. He grabbed the hat, threw it into the air, and kicked it as it came down. He went on kicking it until the straw was in shreds. Still without a word he marched on out of the hall.

"Carrots isn't afraid of anything!" one awe-struck boy said.

Winston didn't turn his head, but he had heard the words. He was satisfied. He had achieved his purpose.

3. At the Bottom of the Class

Probably Winston would have been expelled from that school if his parents hadn't been so well known. The headmaster even tried to please them in his reports about their son. He said once that Winston was "sometimes extremely good" in history and geography. He added, however, that he "has no ambition." He also said he was "troublesome," that he "must treat his work in general more seriously," and that he had the lowest marks in his class.

Winston's own brief letters home, read by the headmaster before they were sent, didn't mention the beatings he regularly received. They didn't say that he often felt sick. His parents learned about that only after he had been at St. George's for about two years. Then he became so ill that he had to be taken home. It was decided to transfer him to a school at the seaside resort of Brighton, where the family doctor could keep an eye on him.

The two elderly ladies who ran the Brighton school shook their heads over Winston's behavior, but they allowed him privileges that made his life bearable. He was even permitted to go riding three times a week. "I make my pony canter," he wrote his mother proudly. He also wrote her about the school plays, in which he often took a leading role, and begged her and his father to come to see them—and to see him. Lady Randolph visited the school for an hour or two, but only rarely. Lord Randolph did not come at all. Once, even though he was staying with friends in Brighton, he did not stop at the school to see his son.

Winston proudly showed his friends pictures of his handsome parents that he cut out of newspapers and magazines. He could also sometimes supply them with autographs of the famous Lord and Lady Randolph.

"Everybody wants your Autograph," he wrote his father. In the same letter, to prove how eagerly he was following his father's political career, he wrote, "The driver of the Electric Railway said 'that Lord R. Churchill would be Prime Minister.' "

The Tories won the election of 1886, and Lord Randolph, hailed as the man most responsible for defeating the Liberals, became his party's leader in the House of Commons. He was named to the cabinet as chancellor of the exchequer. Lord Randolph had reached the peak of a career that would be almost as brief as it was spectacular: when he resigned as chancellor some months later, after a disagreement with other party leaders over the budget, he would never again hold a cabinet post—although his friends would believe for years that he would soon be returned to power. No hint of his decline, however, shadowed his brilliant success immediately after the election. His son read reports of his speeches in the House, even if he could not always understand them, in the hope that someday he would have the chance to discuss them with his father.

During a school vacation at about this time, Lord Randolph walked into the nursery one day and saw Winston arranging his toy soldiers for battle. Winston had more than a thousand of the little figures, some mounted on horseback, all in British uniform. He had marshaled them into an infantry division and a cavalry brigade, complete with miniature guns and gun carriers. He looked up to see his father standing over him with one of his rare smiles.

"Would you like to go into the army, Winston?" Lord Randolph asked.

Winston thought instantly, as he put it long afterward, that "my father, with his experience and flair had discerned in me the qualities of military genius." Suddenly he could imagine himself commanding thousands of real soldiers, like his famous ancestor, the first duke of Marlborough. "Oh, yes!" he said.

Years later he realized that his father had suggested the army as a career only because Lord Randolph had decided his son was not clever enough for the law, or one of the few other professions regarded as suitable for the grandson of a duke.

So Winston's future was decided. When he left Brighton after three years, he entered Harrow, a famous school which prepared most of its students for the great universities of Oxford and Cambridge. Winston was to prepare himself for the military college at Sandhurst.

Winston had done very poorly on the Harrow entrance examinations. Any other boy would have been refused admission on the grades he received. The Harrow headmaster, however, was one of the first teachers to recognize Winston's real possibilities. He admitted him in spite of his poor grades. He then insisted that Winston spend some of his vacations with a tutor, making up work he had failed.

Winston always complained bitterly when he had to give up any of his holidays. He was particularly enraged when he was once sent to France during Christmas to live with a French family in order to improve his French. "I can't tell you what trouble I have had with Winston this last fortnight," Lady Randolph wrote her husband who was away at the time. "He has bombarded me with letters, cursing his fate and every one . . . he makes as much fuss as tho' he were going to Australia for 2 years."

His French did improve, slowly. In spite of his short stature—he never grew tall—he became so good at fencing that he won a cup as school champion. "I was far

Young Winston as a Harrow student

and away first," he reported to his mother. "Absolutely untouched in the finals." He wrote some lively articles for the school paper. His English compositions earned such high marks that another boy hired him to write his, in return for doing Winston's Latin homework. He won a prize for learning 1200 lines of poetry by heart.

When he took the examinations required for entering military college, however, he failed some subjects completely. He failed those examinations a second time too. School examiners, he once complained, "always tried to ask what I did not know. When I would have willingly displayed my knowledge, they sought to expose my ignorance."

He was grimly resigned to the "cramming" course his father decided was necessary. After a brief vacation with his young brother Jack at the country home of one of their aunts, he was to study with an army officer said to be able to prepare any boy to pass the army tests.

Then, one day during that vacation, Jack and a younger cousin challenged Winston to outrun them. "You'll never catch me," he assured them and started off through the pine woods surrounding the house. He had reached a bridge over a deep ravine when he realized that the boys had circled around and were about to close in on him, one from each end of the bridge.

He saw Jack's exultant grin. He saw the tall pines rising out of the ravine, their tops almost level with the bridge. He leaped off the bridge, arms outstretched to grasp the nearest tree. He missed it and fell thirty feet to the bottom of the ravine, crashing through branches on the way.

The terrified younger boys ran for help. Winston was carried to the house where he remained unconscious for three days, close to death from a ruptured kidney. Specialists arrived. His father was summoned. Weeks went by before Winston could leave his bed and return to his books.

The officer in charge of the cramming course despaired over his new student. He declared he had never known a boy whose ignorance of certain subjects was so nearly complete.

"Surely he never went *through* Harrow," the man said. "He must have gone *under* it."

On his third try, at the end of the course, Winston barely managed to pass the examinations. He entered Sandhurst close to the bottom of a class of 150 cadets.

Within weeks he was surprising everyone but himself by his rapid improvement. He had never been happier than when on horseback, and riding was an important part of a cadet's training. Army tactics was for him a fascinating subject and an easy one, after the hours he had spent maneuvering his toy soldiers. As a descendant of the great duke of Marlborough, he had absorbed British military history all his life, and his phenomenal

Winston (at left) and two friends in the uniform of
cadets at the Royal Military College

memory retained anything that interested him. Now he could make use of everything he knew, everything he could do best. He had an air of command, a sense of reckless daring, that made other men naturally accept him as a leader.

He finished his year-and-a-half course a few weeks after his father's death. He left Sandhurst among the top ten in his class.

Almost immediately, with the help of influential friends of his family, he received a lieutenant's commission in the regiment he preferred above all others, the cavalry regiment of the Queen's Fourth Hussars. Its blue and gold dress uniform was magnificent. Winston felt it would make the best possible background for the medals he hoped to be wearing soon. The adventure and excitement of winning those medals on a battle-front had a great appeal to him. Besides, he knew the British public accepted medals as proof of heroism and frequently elected heroes to office.

The military career to which a very young Winston had once looked forward, for its own sake, had now become in his eyes simply a stepping-stone to the world he meant to claim for himself—the world of politics. He intended to make it so completely his own that someday he would fill the post he felt had been unfairly denied to his father. Winston Churchill had begun to think of himself as a future prime minister of England.

4. In Search of a War

Through most of the year 1895 young Lieutenant Churchill trained with the Fourth Hussars. Then the officers of the regiment were given a long leave after which they would sail to India, then a part of the British Empire, for a long tour of duty.

By 1895 Queen Victoria had been on the throne of England for more than half a century. She had brought peace to the largest and richest empire in the world. She believed she had taught the lesson of peace to all civilized mankind.

Never again, most Englishmen agreed, would Western nations indulge in the folly of war. Primitive peoples, they admitted—especially those who had not been brought under the enlightened protection of England —might continue to fight each other in distant parts of the globe. The English were sure, however, that Europeans had faced each other on the battlefield for the last time.

"We were born too late! We'll never see any real fighting!" one of Churchill's friends complained shortly after their leave had begun. Reginald Barnes was also a lieutenant in the hussars. Like other young officers he was convinced that the most exciting experience life could offer a military man was active service at the front during a "real" war. "Perhaps in India we might see a skirmish between two tribes, but that's all," he said. "Why couldn't we have lived early enough to serve under the old duke of Marlborough?"

"We might see some real fighting if we crossed the Atlantic," Churchill told him. "Spain has sent an expeditionary force to her Cuban colony. The Cubans are revolting. Why shouldn't we get ourselves attached to the Spanish forces for a few weeks?"

The idea had been in his mind for days, partly for financial reasons. He could not afford the season of fox hunting most of his fellow officers were enjoying during their leave, and which their superiors approved of as excellent experience for cavalry recruits. He had once believed his parents possessed "limitless riches." He knew now that Lord Randolph had lost money during the last years of his life. Both Churchill's grandfathers, from whom help might have been expected, were now dead. Lady Randolph was not penniless, but her income was not large and she was extravagant.

She did give her son an allowance. He could not have lived without it, for a cavalry lieutenant's pay did not even cover the cost of the horses he had to keep. Churchill's allowance was smaller than that of most hussars, however, and he was as naturally extravagant as his mother. "My tastes are simple," he often said cheerfully. "I like only the best." He also liked to play polo, and this meant he had to buy his own polo ponies. Already he was beginning to wonder how he could repay the debts he owed.

An inexpensive vacation in Cuba therefore seemed to him a wise choice. He thought he might even make the trip pay for itself by writing articles about it for the *Daily Graphic*. His father had written for that London newspaper during a trip he once made to South Africa. Churchill took it for granted that the *Graphic* would be glad to open its columns to Lord Randolph's son.

Money was not the only thing on his mind. He also wanted to prove his courage, to test himself—and perhaps win some notice—on an actual battlefront.

"Do you really think we could go to Cuba?" Barnes was asking.

"I don't see why not," Churchill said. "The English ambassador to Spain is an old friend of my family. I'm certain he could get us permission to join the Spanish forces."

The matter was settled as easily as he had expected. Even the editor of the *Graphic* fell in with his plans and promised to pay him for firsthand accounts of life on the Cuban war front. Soon Churchill and Barnes were setting sail for New York where they could board a steamer for Cuba.

They remained in New York a week, entertained

from the moment of their arrival by old friends of Lady Randolph. When Churchill wrote to his brother, he described Americans with the same word his English grandfather had once used about his American grandfather: he said he found Americans "vulgar."

"I think, mind you," he went on, "that vulgarity is a sign of strength. A great, crude, strong, young people are the Americans—like a boisterous healthy boy . . . who treads on all your sensibilities, perpetrates every possible horror of ill manners—whom neither age nor just tradition inspires with reverence—but who moves about his affairs with a good hearted freshness which may well be the envy of older nations of the earth. Of course," he added, "there are here charming people who are just as refined and cultured as the best in any country in the world . . ."

When they reached Cuba, Churchill and Barnes spent a few days in the capital and then set off for the front. There was rebel sniping along the way and reports of bombing in the neighborhood, but they arrived safely at the Spanish headquarters. There the general greeted them courteously as "distinguished representatives of a great and friendly nation."

The next morning at dawn they rode off with the Spanish forces through rebel-infested forest. Breakfast came some hours later, a long and leisurely meal. Afterward the entire force slept in the shade for several hours, and then marched on again until dusk fell and it was time to camp for the night.

The same routine was followed the next day, and the next. No rebels were sighted. At breakfast on the third day, Churchill was gnawing the drumstick of what he decided must have been a very scrawny chicken when "a ragged volley rang out from the edge of the forest," as he later wrote. "The horse immediately behind me— not my horse—gave a bound," his account continued. "There was excitement and commotion. A party of soldiers rushed to the place whence the volley had been fired, and of course found nothing except a few empty cartridge cases."

He turned to look at the injured horse. Blood was dripping from a wide dark circle on the animal's chestnut flank. Churchill's first reaction was the startled realization that war could actually mean death for the creatures he had always loved so well.

His next thought was that the bullet which had struck the horse had missed his own head by inches.

"I have been under fire for the first time," he told himself solemnly. The day was November 30, his twenty-first birthday. He was relieved to notice that his hands were not shaking. He remembered thankfully that he had had no impulse to run or hide when the shots sounded. He felt it was the best celebration possible for the birthday that made him officially a man.

Only one other minor skirmish took place during the week he and Barnes remained with the Spanish forces. Then, "Spanish honor and our own curiosity alike being satisfied," Churchill wrote, "the column returned to the coast, and we to England."

Back home once more, wearing the medal the Spanish general had pinned to his coat, Churchill found that people were talking about him. Some said, "Enterprising lad. Got himself into Cuba, you know. Ought to go far." Others said he was "pushy," too eager to make his way among older and more experienced men. "This is a pushy age," Churchill told his mother matter-of-factly. "We must push with the best." He had his own private reason, too, for being "in a hurry," as so many people said he was. He felt sure he would die young, as his father had, and he wanted to prove himself "of some use," as he put it, while he could.

It was the British Empire that was in his mind when he talked of being of use. He had been brought up to be loyal to it and to believe that its vast power was a power for good. That loyalty and that belief were now strengthened.

He had gone to Cuba feeling sympathetic toward the rebels, but he wrote on his return that the rebel army, "consisting to a large extent of colored men, is an undisciplined rabble."

He had been somewhat surprised to see how bravely

the Spaniards fought to retain their Cuban colony—as bravely as he assumed Englishmen would fight to retain their own colonies around the world. He had nevertheless decided that Spain did not rule Cuba as wisely as Britain ruled her possessions. He stated in one article that Spanish administration of Cuba was "bad."

His experience in Cuba, in other words, had not only given him the chance to prove his courage under fire, and to earn some reputation—and some money—by his writings. It had also proved, to his satisfaction, the truth of two ideas basic to his thinking: that people who were not white were inferior to those who were; and that Englishmen were the best fitted of all men to govern "inferior" people.

Years later he could look back and say, with a thoughtful smile, "I was brought up in that state of civilization when it was everywhere accepted that men are born unequal." As a youthful lieutenant he saw no need to comment on that state of inequality; like everyone he knew, he simply took it for granted. He also took for granted that it imposed on born aristocrats, like himself, the responsibility to assume a leader's role.

He felt quite ready for that role now. He was on his way to India as part of Her Majesty's forces sent there to carry out what he would describe as England's "high mission to rule these primitive but agreeable races for their welfare and our own."

5. Soldier and Correspondent

The life of the young hussar officers, when they reached their station at Bangalore, in southern India, was not very demanding.

Churchill, Barnes, and a third officer lived together, sharing the rent of their comfortable bungalow and served by the large staff of servants then customary in India: a valet and an assistant valet, two gardeners, three water carriers, four washermen, a watchman, and a groom for each horse and pony they owned.

For an hour and a half early each morning the young officers drilled their men. They put in another hour and a half of duty after breakfast. That completed their day's work.

It was only eleven o'clock by then, but the sun was high and hot. Everyone avoided it by remaining indoors, behind drawn shades, until five o'clock, the most important hour of their day—the hour for the regiment's favorite sport of polo.

Polo, a dangerous game invented in India long ago, had been enthusiastically adopted by India's British conquerors. The hussars had bought the finest string of Arabian polo ponies they could find and played everyday until it was too dark to see the ball. None of them played with more frenzy and spirit than

As a lieutenant in the Fourth Hussars, young Winston was stationed at Bangalore, India.

Churchill. Leaning down from the back of his galloping steed and swinging his mallet with all his strength, he looked, one officer said, "like a man thrashing at a cobra."

Churchill was on the four-man team the hussars chose to represent them in their first tournament—a contest among the various English and Indian regiments of India's southern region. It took place at Hyderabad, just six weeks after the hussars reached India.

The Indian ruler, or *nizam,* of Hyderabad was one of the wealthiest men in the world. He had provided superb mounts for his own polo team, the Golcondas. The hussars found themselves matched against the Golcondas for their first game.

"Hard luck!" an officer from another British regiment said sympathetically. "Those Indian players can beat every British team in the region."

The Golcondas scored three goals almost immediately. The hussars did not let them score again. To the astonishment of a cheering crowd, they won the match nine goals to three.

They continued to win as they met other teams in the games that followed. The tournament ended with the hussars crowned regional champions. No regiment so recently arrived in India had ever won a tournament before. They promised themselves that

Winston (second from left in the second row) was a soccer player with his squadron's team.

someday they would win the all-India championship.

The polo championship, however, did not replace for Churchill the personal goal he had set himself before he left England. In pursuit of it he was hard at work. Everyday, in the long hot hours of the afternoon while his fellow officers dozed or played cards, he studied.

He had realized, during the months he spent in London at the end of his leave, how great were the gaps in his education. When he heard someone mention "the Socratic method," for example, he didn't know what it was. He meant to find out. He was determined to make himself the equal of any young Englishman who, like himself, hoped for a political career but who had been a university student while he was digging trenches at Sandhurst.

He began his self-education with a favorite of his father's, *The Decline and Fall of the Roman Empire,* eight huge volumes by England's famous Edward Gibbon. He went on to the works of another English historian, Thomas Macaulay. Then he asked his mother to send him copies of Parliamentary debates. Two big books of those debates were published each year. He started reading with the year 1870, four years before his own birth. He meant to know exactly how members of the House conducted themselves before he became one of them.

He scribbled comments in the margins of his books as he read. He took notes. He wrote out his own opinion of the subject of each Parliamentary debate, then read the debate itself, and afterward rewrote his opinion if the debaters had convinced him to change his mind.

It was hard work, and he often wished he could abandon it all for action in the field. Action could further his ambition too, he reminded himself. He was eager to increase the small reputation he had made with his *Graphic* reports from Cuba—and he was still hoping for some British medals. Whenever he heard of an English force going on active duty, he tried to join it.

His first success came when he learned that General Sir Bindon Blood was commanding an expedition against revolting Pathan tribes on India's northern border. Churchill telegraphed the general, who was an old family friend, and asked to be assigned to his staff. While he waited for a reply he arranged to send reports from the frontier to the *Pioneer*, an Indian newspaper. With his mother's help he also received an assignment to write "picturesque forcible letters" from the front to the London *Daily Telegraph*.

"Very difficult; no vacancies," the general finally answered, but he added, "Come up as a correspondent; will try to fit you in."

Churchill hastily arranged leave from the Fourth

Hussars and set off. A five-day train journey across India and forty miles in a jouncing pony cart brought him to the general's headquarters. Soon he was riding forth into the region of the fierce Pathan tribesmen with the first of the general's three brigades.

Only an occasional sniper disturbed their steady progress until the second brigade, following two days behind, suffered a full-scale attack. The general ordered the second brigade's commander to pursue the attackers in retaliation. "You may join that brigade if you want to see a fight," he told Churchill.

The next day Churchill accompanied the second brigade into the Mamund valley. The ridges around it, and the valley floor alike, were scattered with mud hut villages. All appeared deserted. Churchill joined a party sent upward along one of the ridges.

The climb was long and arduous, the heat suffocating. The Pathan village at the top was empty and silent. After a time the party's leader decided to withdraw to a lower knoll.

"You stay here to cover us," he said to one officer, and detailed eight Sikhs, or Indian soldiers, to stay with him.

Churchill said he too would stay behind.

He and the nine others had been alone only a few minutes when suddenly the mountain above them erupted with color and sound. White and blue clad figures were bounding down toward them, voices shouting, swords flashing, guns emitting puffs of smoke. Bullets whizzed past Churchill's head as he flattened himself on the bare earth and took aim at the swiftly moving targets.

Suddenly an officer from the group that had just departed was beside him. "Come on back," the officer ordered. "There's no time to lose."

As the members of the little party rose to their feet, bullets still screaming past them, Churchill saw the officer behind him "spinning around . . . his face a mass of blood, his right eye cut out." Three men in the group had been wounded in that brief moment. Two others were dead.

Churchill helped pick up the wounded men and staggered with them down the ridge. They were under constant fire.

No British troops were waiting for them on the knoll they had been heading for. They could only keep on going.

One wounded British officer was dropped by his terrified carriers when half a dozen Pathan swordsmen rushed at them from behind a house. An instant later a tribesman was slashing at the helpless officer with his sword.

·"I forgot everything else at this moment except a desire to kill this man," Churchill wrote afterward. "I wore my long cavalry sword well sharpened. After all, I had won the Public Schools fencing medal. I resolved on personal combat. . . . The savage saw me coming. . . . He picked up a big stone and hurled it at me with his left hand, and then awaited me, brandishing his sword. There were others waiting not far behind him. I changed my mind about the cold steel. I pulled out my revolver, took, as I thought, most careful aim, and fired. No result. I fired again. No result. I fired again. Whether I hit him or not I cannot tell. At any rate he ran back two or three yards and plumped down behind a rock. The fusillade was continuous. I looked around. I was all alone with the enemy. Not a friend was to be seen. I ran as fast as I could. There were bullets everywhere. I got to the first knoll. Hurrah, there were the Sikhs holding the lower one! They made vehement gestures, and in a few moments I was among them."

The day was not yet over. Even at the foot of the ridge the British were still in danger from Pathans closing steadily in on them. All they could do was huddle in a semi-circle around their wounded and fire steadily at the attackers until finally a large force arrived to relieve them.

Before he was called back to his own regiment Churchill had several other opportunities to see "some real tough fighting." General Blood even used Churchill temporarily as a regimental officer for the Thirty-first Punjab Infantry. "He is working away equal to two ordinary subalterns," Blood declared. Blood could not obtain a medal for his young friend, but in his military dispatches he praised the "courage and resolution" of Lieutenant Churchill, "who made himself useful at a critical moment."

Churchill reported all the frontier action he had seen to the *Daily Telegraph*. He was proud of his letters to the paper. As he wrote his mother, he had taken "the very greatest pains with the style and composition" of them. He was furious when he discovered they had been printed as "by a young officer" rather than over his signature. He immediately decided to use them as the basis for a book on which he could put his own name. He finished it in five weeks and sent it to his mother, who had already made arrangements for it to be published.

Churchill had asked an uncle to check the manuscript for him. He blamed the uncle for what he called "the gross and fearful blunders" in the printed book. He admitted he too was at fault, however, for having been in too much of a hurry to check everything himself.

Many readers noticed the errors. One reviewer said the book had "the punctuation of an idiot or of a school-boy in the lowest form." The same reviewer nevertheless called it a "literary phenomenon" which corrections could transform into "a military classic."

The Prince of Wales wrote Churchill a kind letter about the book and sent a copy of it to his sister, the empress of Germany. Lord Salisbury, the prime minister, admired the book so much that he invited Churchill to visit him on his next leave in London.

Churchill saw to it that he had a leave soon and went to London in spite of the high cost of the journey. He visited the prime minister, who kept him at his side for a long talk.

"I hope you will allow me to say how much you remind me of your father," the elderly statesman said. "If there is anything at any time that I can do which would be of assistance to you," he added, "pray do not fail to let me know."

Churchill took quick advantage of the offer. For months he had been hoping to join the forces then fighting in Egypt, where England was trying to establish authority over fierce Dervish tribesmen.

"Would you help me get to Egypt?" Churchill asked Lord Salisbury.

A few days later he received the word he had been hoping for. The War Office was ordering him to "report at once at the Abassiyeh Barracks, Cairo." He had been assigned to the Twenty-first Lancers.

Once more Churchill asked for and obtained leave

from his own regiment. Once more he arranged to write newspaper stories from the front, this time at a higher rate than he had been paid before. Within days he was with the troops moving up the Nile River toward the great city of Khartoum, the Dervish stronghold.

At Omdurman, on the riverbank opposite Khartoum, the Dervish force of 60,000 men was sighted. Slowly, in a line several miles long, it moved toward the 20,000 British troops. Most of the Dervish were armed with spears and scimitars. The British cavalry carried swords, but the larger number of the men—the infantrymen —had rifles, and the British army was supported by heavy guns drawn up at its rear.

"The enemy came on like the sea," Churchill wrote, describing what he saw from a hill where he had been stationed as a scout. "I saw the full blast of Death strike this human wall," he went on. "Down went their standards by dozens and their men by hundreds. . . . One saw them jumping and tumbling under the shrapnel bursts; but none turned back."

Only after the first great clash was Churchill in action himself. Then he led his troop forward as the regiment of lancers advanced over the hard sand toward "a long line of blue-black objects." The objects proved to be rifle-armed foes.

The lancers' trumpet sounded "Trot!"

This painting illustrates the cavalry charge of the Twenty-first Lancers against the Dervish at Omdurman. Churchill participated in the battle.

Then it sounded once again, "Right wheel into line!"

"The regiment broke into a gallop," Churchill wrote afterward, "and the 21st Lancers were committed to their first charge in war!"

It was Churchill's first charge too. In training maneuvers, at the command to charge, he would raise his sword and "could hardly help shouting in joyous wrath," he once wrote. Now he was cooler. Sometime earlier he had wrenched a shoulder that had since given him trouble, and he knew he would not be able to use his sword effectively. Somehow, as he galloped on, he managed to sheath it and to take out and cock the pistol he had purchased in London before he left.

"One really had not time to be frightened," he remembered later.

Directly in front of him he saw two men in blue a few yards apart. They both fired as he rode between them. He passed beyond them unhurt.

When the pony he was riding slid down into a shallow sandy hollow, he found himself surrounded by dozens of the enemy. He rode up on the opposite slope, unharmed.

Dervishes were scattering everywhere in front of him. One threw himself at the feet of Churchill's mount, curved sword thrust at the pony's legs. Churchill turned the animal aside and fired two shots into the man's body.

Immediately another figure appeared before him, sword upraised. Churchill fired at such close range that his pistol itself struck the blue-robed Dervish before the man fell.

The whole action lasted only a few minutes. Several more times Churchill fired at men who were themselves aiming directly at him. By the time he had emptied his pistol, it was all over. He had not been injured even slightly.

The rest of his regiment were less fortunate. Of approximately 300 men, 70 had been killed or wounded, and 120 horses had been lost.

The defeat of the Dervish army, however, was complete. Thousands of dead bodies—one-third of the whole Dervish force of 60,000—lay on the great sandy plain where the battle of Omdurman had taken place.

Churchill took the bloody memory of that carnage home with him when the lancers were sent back to England a few days later. Another of his vivid memories was the sight of English soldiers slaying their wounded enemies in cold blood. He meant to mention both sights in *The River War*, a new book he was planning about England's role in Egypt. If his frankness about British brutality stirred up some quarrels, he wouldn't mind. Arguments about the work could only make his name better known and perhaps add to the sale of the book. This time, however, he was going to be very careful and take his time. He didn't want to publish another book that was full of errors.

He had another volume almost ready for the printer too—a novel he had been writing in his spare time during the past few years. Its hero was an ambitious young statesman who made fiery speeches and who was willing to give his life to free his people from the rule of a dictator. Churchill was not very satisfied with his beautiful heroine, Lucile. When his grandmother read his manuscript, she had written him, "It is clear you have not yet attained a knowledge of Women—and it is evident you have (I am thankful to see) no experience of Love!"

Churchill's ambition had indeed left him little time for romance, but he still hoped that *Savrola*, as he called his novel, would interest both men and women and thus win him more of the fame and money he now needed immediately. He had decided that as soon as he had helped the Fourth Hussars compete for the all-India polo championship, he would resign his army commission and make his formal entry into politics.

With this plan in mind he visited the national headquarters of the Conservative party before returning to India. He wanted to let the party leaders know that he would soon be available to run—or to stand, in the British phrase—for a seat in the House of Commons.

He hoped they would then spread the news among local groups seeking a candidate for the next election. (In British politics a candidate may stand for Parliament anywhere in the country; he is not restricted to the locality where he himself lives and votes.)

"I think we can easily find you a seat, lieutenant," the party manager said. "Will you be able to make a fairly large contribution to any local party which chooses you as a candidate?"

"I'm afraid not," Churchill told him. "It will be all I can do to pay my own expenses."

"I see." The manager was thoughtful. "Well," he said finally, "in that case we shall probably not be able to find you a 'safe' seat—one where election is almost certain. But we shall see what we can do. Of course your father's name will help you," he added, "and your military experience."

Suddenly Churchill noticed a large book labeled "Speakers Wanted."

"Tell me about this," he said. "Do you mean there are a lot of meetings which *want* speakers?"

"Dozens of them," the manager assured him. "Would you like to make a speech somewhere?"

"Anywhere," Churchill said.

Together they selected a political fund-raising garden party to be held in the town of Bath ten days later. Churchill spent most of that time working on his speech.

In the train on the way to Bath he met a reporter for the *Morning Post.*

"I'm being sent down to report on the first political speech by the late Lord Randolph's son," the newspaperman said.

Churchill grinned. "I'm Winston Churchill," he said. They were friends before the journey's end.

Many activities were taking place that afternoon at the big estate where the garden party was held. There were children's races, games of skill, and stands selling refreshments.

Churchill eyed the cheerful crowd. "They don't look much interested in politics," he muttered.

At five o'clock a bell rang, and an announcer summoned those present to a tent where a small speaker's platform had been set up. The tent was still only partly filled when the chairman introduced Churchill.

"We are fortunate to have with us today," he said, "the son of Lord Randolph Churchill, one of the greatest leaders the Conservative party has ever had. Lieutenant Churchill's bravery with the sword and his brilliancy with the pen is, I am sure, known to you all." The chairman stepped aside.

It was time for Churchill to speak. He knew he had a slight speech impediment—a faint lisp, some of his friends called it. He hoped it would not be too noticeable. He cleared his throat and told his first joke.

The audience laughed. He told another and people laughed more loudly.

The crowd before him grew, as the sound of laughter drew others into the tent.

Churchill made what he thought was one of his strongest points. The crowd cheered!

From then on he enjoyed himself. "I can really do it!" he was thinking. "It's easy!"

That evening he returned to London with the news-paperman, who had offered to take him to his office and let him see his finished story.

"If you find anything wrong," the reporter said, when he handed the story over, "feel free to correct it."

Churchill saw immediately that it was long enough to fill a whole newspaper column. He smiled as he read it, thinking of the thousands of others who would be reading it in the morning.

Suddenly he picked up a pencil and crossed out the word "cheers," which the reporter had written after one of Churchill's most enthusiastically received remarks.

The reporter protested. "But the crowd did cheer!"

"I know," Churchill agreed, and over the one word he had crossed out, he wrote four others: "loud and prolonged applause."

An editor, looking over Churchill's shoulder at that moment, later told his friends, "I knew right then that this chap would amount to something!"

6. Off to Another War

Winston Churchill sailed for India once more at the end of 1898. He was back in England in less than six months.

During that half year he had led the Fourth Hussars to victory in the all-India inter-regimental polo tournament, making three of the four goals in the final match. Churchill left the hussars in a blaze of glory.

Several groups in England had shown interest in making him their candidate at the next general election which would take place in eighteen months. (British general elections then occurred every seven years—the interval was later changed to five years—although the party in power could then, as now, call for an election at any time by dissolving the existing Parliament.) One of the groups interested in Churchill represented the Tories of the thriving cotton-spinning town of Oldham. Churchill was flattered by their enthusiasm for him. He was also impatient at having to wait so long to enter upon his political career.

Suddenly one of Oldham's two Tory members of Parliament died. The other resigned. A special election, or by-election, was called in Oldham, and Churchill was asked to stand as one of the pair of Tory candidates who would oppose two candidates of the Liberal party. His running mate was to be a well-known leader of the cotton-spinners union, a staunch Tory who nevertheless held many socialist views.

Voters were amused to see a trade-unionist with a leaning toward socialism on the same ballot with a young descendant, or scion, of one of England's noble families. "The Scion and the Socialist," they called the pair, and came out in large numbers to hear their vigorous campaign.

Some of them cheered Churchill when he said that he himself would not have voted for a bill which the Tories had recently backed in Parliament, a bill to which many of the people of Oldham objected. Tory leaders were troubled to learn that he was so ready to oppose the stand of his own party.

Oldham certainly did not offer the two Tories "safe" seats. The Liberal candidates were extremely popular and had seemingly unlimited funds. As the campaign wore on, Churchill realized that the Liberals were almost certain to win unless a miracle occurred.

There was no miracle. Churchill and his running mate lost the election.

"Never mind," Arthur Balfour, Tory leader of the House of Commons wrote Churchill kindly, ". . . this small reverse will have no permanent ill effect upon your political fortunes." At the same time, however,

Balfour was commenting to his friends about Churchill's stand against the Tory-backed bill. "I thought he was a young man of promise, but it appears he is a young man of promises," Balfour said.

Churchill was not yet twenty-five. He had already given members of his party reason to eye him with the same kind of mistrust they had once shown of his outspoken and independent father. He had also established a reputation which those party leaders could not ignore. One proof of it was a *Daily Mail* article about him, called "The Youngest Man in Europe," by a brilliant journalist, George W. Steevens.

"In years he is a boy," Steevens had written, "in temperament he is also a boy; but in intention, in deliberate plan, purpose, adaptation of means to ends he is already a man. . . . With ambitions fixed, with the steps toward their attainment clearly defined with a precocious, almost uncanny judgement. . ."

He wrote that Churchill had "qualities which might make him, almost at will, a great popular leader, a great journalist, or the founder of a great advertising business. . ."

"What he will become, who shall say?" Steevens asked. "At the rate he goes there will hardly be room for him in Parliament at thirty or in England at forty."

Two months after the Oldham election a long-simmering quarrel in southern Africa seemed to be coming to a head. Churchill had been following it with great interest.

England had two colonies there, the Cape Colony and Natal. Both had originally been settled by the Dutch. When England took them over, many of their Boer inhabitants—cattle-farming descendants of the early Dutch—had trekked northward in search of freedom. Eventually they had established two inland republics of their own, the Transvaal and the Orange Free State. Then the discovery of gold in those republics had brought in a flood of fortune-seekers, mostly British. Fearful of once again coming under British domination, the Boers had taxed the newcomers but refused them citizenship and voting rights.

The new British residents of the Boer republic insisted, in words American colonists had once used, that they would not accept "taxation without representation." At their request British troops took up positions along the republic's borders. The Boers demanded that the troops be withdrawn. The British refused to leave. With each passing day open conflict seemed more likely.

Suddenly Churchill received an offer from the London *Daily Mail* to go to South Africa as its correspondent there. Churchill reported the offer to his earlier employer, the *Morning Post*, and said he would write for the *Post* instead for a salary of £250, or about $1,000 a month plus full expenses. Probably no reporter had ever before demanded such high pay. The *Post* nevertheless agreed to his terms. He sailed for Africa on October 14, 1899, two days after war between the British and the Boers had been officially declared.

The many officers and correspondents on board with him feared the excitement would all be over before they arrived. They did not believe the militarily untrained Boers could long withstand British military might. When they reached the Cape Colony, after a two-week voyage, they were staggered to learn that the British had met defeat on almost every hand. The Boers had invaded both the Cape Colony and Natal and were besieging a major city in each: Ladysmith in Natal and Mafeking in the Cape Colony.

Determined to reach the front immediately, Churchill and a few other correspondents hurried to Durban and left that port by what proved to be the last inland-bound train. At the little station of Estcourt the train was halted. The line beyond Estcourt, the soldiers stationed there said, had been seized by the Boers.

"There was nothing to do but wait," Churchill wrote.

He had brought along a valet and a supply of his favorite wines. When he and his correspondent tent-mate had hired a cook, they were ready to serve dinner each evening to the officers stranded there with them.

Each morning scouting parties of cavalrymen went out into the surrounding hills to make certain no Boer forces were about to descend on the town. Nothing occurred that made exciting copy for the *Morning Post*.

On the evening of the seventh day Captain Aylmer Haldane, whom Churchill had known in India, drew him quietly aside.

"The general has an idea for a new kind of scouting party," Haldane said. "He wants me to make up an armored train and take it on up the line tomorrow."

Churchill stared at him. "He still underestimates the enemy, doesn't he?" he said. "What makes him think the Boers won't just let the train go by and then dynamite the tracks behind it so that it can't return here?"

"The same question had occurred to me," Haldane

Churchill was a British newspaper correspondent in South Africa, reporting on the Boer War, when this picture was taken.

said grimly. "But I've been given my orders. Do you want to come along?" he added.

"Certainly I'll come," Churchill said.

Under a rainy sky the six-car train set off the next morning at dawn. Five of the cars were armored and carried guns and men of the Dublin fusiliers and the Durban light infantry. The one ordinary car carried railway repairmen and equipment. The engine and its little coal-bearing tender were in the middle of the train, pushing three cars and pulling the other three.

For fourteen miles, all the way to the little Chieveley station, the train moved through empty hilly country. No Boers were sighted. Haldane reported his position to the general through the station's telegraph office.

A moment later the Englishmen saw figures on the hill above the track they had just come over.

"Boers," Haldane said briefly. "Start back immediately," he ordered the engineer, "before they can get down to the track and cut us off."

The train moved an instant later, heading back toward Estcourt.

It was chugging around the foot of the hill when gunfire sounded from the group of men still on the hill's crest, and a burst of shrapnel struck the rearmost open-topped car in which Churchill and Haldane were riding. The train was starting down a steep grade, and its wheels were spinning faster now. Within a few more moments, Churchill realized, they would be out of range of the Boers' fire.

Suddenly there was a crash. Churchill and Haldane and the other men in the car were knocked off their feet and thrown forward. The train slammed to a halt.

Shaken but unhurt, the men in the rear car pulled themselves up. Shots were steadily whizzing overhead. A quick glance over the side of the car showed Churchill that the Boers on the hill were now moving down toward the track, taking shelter behind bushes and firing as they came.

"Will you go up ahead and see what's happened?" Haldane asked Churchill.

Haldane then issued orders to the fusiliers to ready the one naval gun they carried. Churchill left the car, on the side away from the shooting, and hurried forward behind the partial protection of the train.

The three cars ahead of the engine had all been derailed. Only one had been thrown clear of the tracks. The two closest to the engine—one upright, one on its side—were at angles to the rail line and formed a barrier which the engine and the cars could not pass.

Wounded men were crawling or staggering out of the cars, seeking shelter.

The engineer was climbing down from his cab, his face bloody, his eyes dazed. "I'm getting out of here!" he was muttering.

Churchill took command. "You can't do that," he told the engineer firmly. "You're the only man who can drive the engine."

"But I'm a civilian!" the engineer said. "Nobody pays me to be a target!"

"Don't you know nobody ever gets hit twice on the same day?" Churchill demanded, inventing the folklore he felt the occasion required. "You're safe now! And when will you ever have such a chance to be rewarded for distinguished gallantry—for carrying on your duty while wounded and under fire? Think of the opportunity, man!"

"Well—"the engineer said dubiously. Then he added, "But the engine can't go anywhere with those cars on the rails."

"We're going to get them off," Churchill said, and turned to the soldiers and railway repairmen who were crawling out of the derailed cars.

"Come on, men!" he said. "We have work to do."

For the next hour he was everywhere, rallying the uninjured men to tasks they would not have thought themselves capable of. He used their manpower, and the power of the engine, to push and pull at the derailed cars in an effort to clear the tracks.

Always there were bullets streaking toward them from the Boers, secure in their protected positions. Always there were the groans of the wounded, lying helpless on the wet ground in the rain. Churchill ignored the bullets and seemed not to hear the groans.

"Think what a great story this will be!" he said when the men seemed too exhausted for another effort. "All right now! Let's have the engine full speed ahead this time, and I think it will jam its way past that corner of the car!"

The three cars behind the engine had been detached and moved backward along the track to make it easier for the engine to maneuver. The engineer backed up and then drove hard forward. This time the engine pushed the last metal obstacle out of its way and rode free beyond it.

"You did it!" Churchill congratulated him. "Now let's drag the other three cars up here and recouple them to the engine."

But the weight of the vehicles defeated the men. By now the fire from the Boers' guns was more furious than before.

"Let's load the wounded men aboard the engine and its tender and let the engineer get under way with them," Churchill suggested. "He can go slowly, and the rest of the men can run alongside, in the shelter of the engine."

Haldane agreed. Churchill helped the wounded aboard. There were so many of them by now that both the cab of the engine and the tender were tightly jammed by the suffering men. Churchill was beside the engineer when he gave the order to go forward. The engine began to move.

A few moments later Churchill realized that Haldane and the rest of the men were being left behind.

"Cross that bridge up ahead and wait for us on the far side," Churchill told the engineer. Then he leaped off the cab and started back toward the lagging soldiers.

Suddenly two men in wide-brimmed hats and dark clothes appeared a hundred yards away from him, their guns aimed straight at him. Churchill spun around and ran in the opposite direction. Bullets missed him by inches.

He was in a narrow, steeply-banked railroad cut that was like a trap. He scrambled up one bank and crouched in a hollow, his eyes searching for cover.

What he saw was a grim-faced bearded horseman almost on top of him, aiming a rifle at his head.

Churchill knew that if he moved the man would fire. And he knew that at such short range the rifleman could not miss.

At long last the luck that had carried him through so many dangers seemed to have deserted him. He had escaped Indian bullets and Dervish sword blades by a hair's breadth. This time he could not escape.

Slowly he rose to his feet and raised his arms above his head. With a sense of amazement that disaster could actually befall him, he surrendered to the enemy.

7. Prisoner of the Boers

Churchill's captor nodded briefly at him and gestured in the direction he wanted him to move. Churchill walked back along the line toward the little Chieveley station, the horseman at his heels.

Together they approached a group of men, whom Churchill recognized as Haldane and his fusiliers, surrounded by Boers. They too had been captured.

In long silent lines, closely guarded on either side, they were all marched off on a three-day journey to the Boer capital, Pretoria.

With time to think it over as they walked, Churchill realized that the engineer and the Durban infantrymen would report the whole story to the correspondents at Estcourt. "It will be in all the papers, you know," he told Haldane. "We'll be heroes!" Reminding himself how much English voters admired heroes, he decided that to be captured was not necessarily a disaster after all.

In Pretoria, Churchill and Haldane, separated from the enlisted men, were quartered in a building that had served as a school before the outbreak of war. Other previously captured officers were already imprisoned there. They were made fairly comfortable and allowed to exercise on the school grounds, which were surrounded by a high corrugated iron fence.

Immediately they began to consider possible means of escape. At the same time Churchill formally petitioned for his own release on the grounds that he was a civilian.

"But you were not behaving as a civilian at the time of your capture," a Boer official reminded him, not ill-naturedly. "If it had not been for you, we understand, the men who got away on that engine would now be our prisoners too." Then another Boer official added, "We're not going to let you go, old chappie, even if you

Taken captive by the Boers, Winston (far right) was imprisoned in Pretoria, South Africa.

are a correspondent. We don't catch the son of a lord every day."

One escape plan after another was made and discarded. Churchill's own favorite, involving all the inmates of the prison, was to disarm their guards, lock them up, free the enlisted men from their own prison nearby, and then all together assault and seize the Boers' capital. From that stronghold, Churchill pointed out, they might negotiate a peaceful settlement of the whole war. "It was a great dream," Churchill wrote afterward. Even he was finally forced to agree that it was also greatly impractical.

Eventually he and Haldane and a third man, who knew the language and the geography of the country, settled upon a daring but simple plan. It was based on the fact that a circular latrine stood against the high fence. Once inside the latrine, the prisoners believed, it would be possible to climb the fence in a brief moment when the guards had their backs turned.

The prisoners tried unsuccessfully to put their plan into operation on the night of December 11, almost a month after their capture. The next night they tried again. First Haldane and Churchill went into the latrine, decided a sentry would see any move they made, and left. Next Churchill tried going into the latrine alone.

Through a chink in the latrine wall he watched the sentry. Suddenly the man turned to light his pipe.

Churchill sprang instantly onto a ledge, reached for the top of the fence, scrambled over it, and dropped down into the garden on the other side. In the scanty shelter of a few leafless bushes, he crouched there waiting for the others to join him.

The minutes ticked by. Boer officers walked past him, sometimes at a distance of only a few yards. Each time someone approached he held his breath.

At the end of an hour, which had seemed to him far longer than that, he heard a tapping on the fence against which he was huddled. He put his ear against it. Faintly Haldane's voice came through to him.

"We can't make it," Haldane whispered. "They're watching. Can you get back in?"

"No," Churchill whispered, after a painful moment's thought. There was no ledge on the outside of the fence. He would have to leap for the top of the barrier, and he knew that would make enough noise to attract attention.

"I'll have to go on alone," he concluded.

"Well, good luck," Haldane whispered. "We'll try to cover for you until morning," he added.

Churchill took a deep breath. Feeling certain that he would be caught within minutes, he rose to his feet and marched boldly toward a gate that opened onto the road. He was wearing a brown flannel civilian suit he had bought when the Boers permitted him to cash a check, and a black hat with a wide curled brim. Tilting the hat brim to shield his face and humming a tune, he walked straight past a sentry stationed on the road. Still humming, he went on through street after street until he found himself outside the city in open country.

One of the few things he knew about the area was that a railroad ran from Pretoria to the safety of Portuguese East Africa, 300 miles away. Since the compass and the map he and his friends had planned to use were not in his possession—the only supplies he carried were four slabs of chocolate—he decided the railroad line was the one guide he could follow.

Eventually he found the tracks, tried to judge by the stars the direction he should take, and started off between the rails. As he walked, he made up his mind to hide near a station and board the first freight train that stopped there. He would leave it before dawn, conceal himself during the day, and ride another freight the next night. By this method, he hoped, he would reach Portuguese territory without being caught.

His plan worked that night. He rode a freight until nearly dawn, kept out of sight of wandering Boer herdsmen by hiding in a wood until dark, and then sought out another station near which he waited for a second train. Hours went by. None appeared. At last he was forced to conclude that this section of the line was unused at night.

Close to despair now, he again started to walk along

the tracks. His progress was painfully slow. Often he had to detour far around small lighted stations or herdsmen's campfires close to the line.

Suddenly he saw some lights at a distance from the tracks and decided they must indicate a settlement of Kaffirs, the aborigines of the area. He had been told that Kaffirs hated the Boers. If he showed them his English money and asked them in sign language for food and shelter, he thought there might be a good chance that they would be willing to help him.

Heading through the dark toward the lights, which seemed farther away the longer he walked, he found himself lost in a bog. He was soaked to the waist before he emerged on its far side.

He turned back then, but only briefly. He could imagine no hope of aid in the direction from which he had come.

When at last he drew near the lights, he saw, instead of the Kaffir huts he had expected, several buildings around the mouth of a coal mine. One of the buildings was a small two-story stone house.

He hesitated. It seemed to him more than likely that the house was occupied by Boers. Was it possible that even Boers might help him, he wondered, if he gave them all the money he carried and promised them a great deal more? He didn't know. All he was sure of was that he was now far from the railroad tracks and that daylight would come soon. If he didn't try for help at the house, he didn't know what else he could do.

He walked up to the door and banged on it.

He banged again.

An upper window opened and a man's voice demanded, *"Wer ist da?"*

Churchill recognized the language as Dutch. His impulse was to run. Instead he stood his ground and called out, "I want help. I have had an accident."

The window was shut. Footsteps sounded inside. The door opened.

The man who faced him now spoke English, as Churchill had done. "What do you want?" he asked.

Churchill had no idea of how he would answer the question until he heard himself say he was a farmer on his way to join the Boer forces and that he had fallen off a train.

"I have been unconscious for hours," he added.

The man looked at him carefully. "Come in," he said finally. He showed Churchill into a dark room, lit a lamp, and put down the revolver he had been holding. "I think I'd like to know a little more about this railway accident of yours," he said.

"I think I had better tell you the truth," Churchill said. "I am Winston Churchill, war correspondent for the *Morning Post*. I escaped last night from Pretoria. I have plenty of money. Will you help me?"

Again the man stared at him. Then he moved to the door of the room and, as Churchill eyed him fearfully, he locked it.

Suddenly the man came straight toward Churchill, hand outstretched. "Thank God you came here!" he said. "This is the only house within twenty miles where you would not be handed over to the Boers. We are all English here. We will see you through."

The man then quickly introduced himself as John Howard, manager of the mine. He and three other British employes had been left in charge of it, with the understanding that they remain neutral during the hostilities. While Churchill was given food and drink, Howard and the other men worked out a plan for concealing their guest from the Boer police, who were already searching for him throughout the area.

At first Churchill was reluctant to agree to their scheme. He feared the Englishmen would be jailed on his account. They were determined, however, to see that he reached safety. One of them, Dan Dewsnap, crushed Churchill's hand in a warm grip. He came from Oldham, the town where Churchill had lost the election not many weeks before. "They'll all vote for you next time," Dewsnap assured him.

For the next two days Churchill was hidden in a small rat-infested chamber carved out of the earth, far down at the bottom of the mine. Howard traveled twenty miles to the home of a friend to get food for him, explaining that he dared take nothing more from their own kitchen for fear of arousing the suspicion of the Dutch servants. On the third day, assured that the search for him had moved to another region, Churchill was moved to a small unused office above ground.

On the morning of December 19 Howard opened the door of that office and beckoned Churchill to follow him. Together they crossed to a railroad siding where Kaffirs were loading three freight cars with bags of wool. Howard had told Churchill that a neighbor, who had been brought into the conspiracy, was shipping his wool to the Portuguese port of Lourenço Marques that day.

Howard pointed to a tunnel hollowed out of the wool bales piled in one car. Churchill squeezed into it and crawled through to the center of the car, where he found an open space large enough for him to lie down in. There was food and drink in his tiny cell, and a revolver. Three hours later he heard an approaching engine and felt the jerk and bump of the car as it was coupled to the train. The wheels under him began to turn. He slept finally, woke, and slept again.

Late the next afternoon the train stopped at what he thought must be Komati Poort, a Boer town on the Portuguese East Africa border. Lying perfectly still, he listened until almost midnight to the sounds of tramping footsteps and Dutch-speaking voices. He hoped they belonged to customs men. He knew they might belong instead to Boer police searching for him.

At last he felt the car moving once more. He peered through a chink between the bales as soon as it was light. The first station sign he saw was in Portuguese.

Thrusting the bales of wool aside and pushing his head above them into the empty, friendly air, he opened his mouth wide and, as he wrote later, "sang and shouted and crowed at the top of my voice."

That same afternoon the train reached Lourenco Marques. Churchill had already cleaned his hiding place so that no one could ever guess it had been occupied. He moved through the tunnel between the bales and peered carefully out of the car. Waiting for a moment when no one was looking in his direction, he stepped out onto the tracks. Confident that, in his rumpled clothes, he looked like a workman himself, he walked boldly through the station and found his way to the British consulate.

He knocked on the door. The irritated clerk who opened it said immediately that the consul could see no one.

"Come to his office tomorrow," he ordered, eyeing Churchill's clothes and unshaven face with open disdain. "And now be off!"

"I insist upon seeing the consul!" Churchill said loudly as the door closed. "I insist upon seeing him personally!"

Suddenly another man was peering at him through the window beside the door. That same man, a moment later, was reopening the door and asking Churchill's name. It was the consul himself. He drew Churchill into the security of the building.

Churchill learned immediately that his escape had been widely reported by the newspapers. England had suffered further and disastrous defeats while he was being held in Pretoria, and Englishmen everywhere had seized upon his achievement as the first British triumph in many weeks.

Waiting only long enough to enjoy a bath and a good meal, to acquire new clothes, and send off a batch of cables, Churchill boarded a ship heading that same night for Durban, the city he had left at the beginning of his adventure.

For the next six months he remained in Africa, knowing that every dispatch he sent home now would be read by people to whom he had already become famous. He did not simply report what he saw. As had become his habit, he also commented on the conduct of the war. "More irregular corps are wanted. Are the gentlemen of England all fox-hunting?" one of his *Morning Post* stories demanded. He did not repent such impudent questions even when he received a cable from London which said, "Best friends here hope you won't go making further ass of yourself."

Soon after his well-publicized escape from the Boers, young Churchill became a popular public figure. Here he adresses a crowd in Durban.

With his usual ability to seek out the liveliest action, Churchill took part in the skirmishes and battles which finally resulted in lifting the siege of Ladysmith. Afterward he joined in the long march to Pretoria, riding comfortably in the well-stocked wagon his expense account provided. As one of the first Englishmen to enter the Boers' capital, he went immediately to the

prison where some of the men he had known there—
Haldane had successfully escaped—were still being held.
He was present when they joyfully locked their former
guards in the cells, tore down the Boer flag, and ran up
the British flag in its place.

When he finally set sail for home, he had already
finished one book about the Boer War and started another. His *The River War* had received excellent reviews
while he was away. Even his novel had been praised. It
was his newspaper reports, however, which had won
him such a wide reputation that he was the subject of a
popular song:

> *You've heard of Winston Churchill;*
> *This is all I need to say—*
> *He's the latest and the greatest*
> *Correspondent of the day.*

He was welcomed on his arrival in England as the
hero he had deliberately set out to be, and for which his
ebullient nature so well fitted him.

Now he could even make fun of the Boer poster which
had described him as a wanted man "about 5 ft. 8″ or 9″,
blonde with light thin small moustache, walks with slight
stoop, cannot speak any Dutch, during long conversa-
tions he occasionally make a rattling noise in his throat."
What had most offended him about the poster was that

it offered a reward for him, dead or alive, of only £25, or about $125. His fellow Englishmen, Churchill was cheerfully certain, had come to value him at considerably more than that.

Proofs of his popularity were in the great pile of mail that was waiting for him. He took special satisfaction in the letter of an officer he had met in Africa, who wrote, "I feel certain that I shall someday shake hands with you as prime minister of England."

Early in September Parliament was dissolved, and a general election was called. Eager to take his first important political step without further delay, Churchill considered the twelve offers that he received to stand for election to the House of Commons. In spite of the fact that he knew he would be facing long odds there, he decided to accept once more the offer from Oldham.

The Tories of Oldham greeted him with wild enthusiasm when he arrived among them. In his first address to them he told the story of his escape, and mentioned that it had been an Oldham man who helped to conceal his presence in the mine shaft and aided him to safety.

"His wife's in the gallery!" someone shouted.

The cheers were deafening then. The evening was a gloriously emotional success.

Churchill knew the strength of the Liberal opposition, however. He worked harder in the campaign than he had ever worked in his life.

When the citizens of Oldham went to the polls, some Liberals divided their votes. Thus, although Churchill's running mate was defeated, those Liberals and his own Tory supporters elected him to the House of Commons.

He was twenty-five years old. He had spent his twenty-fifth birthday in prison, fretful over the time he was wasting there. He had come a long distance since then. He felt he was on his way at last toward the great goal he had set himself.

8. Political Rebel

Winston Churchill felt at home the moment he walked into the House of Commons and took the seat his father had once occupied.

All around him were men who, like himself, had been elected to represent the "common" people of England. In the nearby House of Lords, the second House of England's Parliament, sat the peers of the realm representing England's noble families and the official Church of England. Churchill had known members of both Houses since his boyhood. Some of them were related to him. His friend and cousin George—everyone called him Sunny—had been sitting in the House of Lords since he had become the ninth duke of Marlborough not long before.

Now Churchill himself had become part of the government which he firmly believed was not only the strongest, but also the finest government in the world.

He was entering Parliament in what was in many ways a new era. The twentieth century, which seemed so full of promise for the betterment of mankind, was only a year old. The long reign of Queen Victoria had finally ended with her death, and now her son, King Edward VII, sat on the throne.

A new party had recently appeared on the political

stage—the Labor party, made up largely of the organized workers of increasingly industrial England. Its representatives in Parliament had already broken the old pattern of a two-party House, divided between Tories, or Conservatives, and Liberals.

For Churchill it was also a new era in a more personal way: he had become financially independent. Between his election and his first appearance in Parliament he had toured England, Canada, and the United States, speaking about his war experiences. His lecture fees and the earnings from his books and other writings added up to £10,000—10,000 British pounds, a sum then equivalent to $50,000.

"I am vy proud," he wrote in a typically abbreviated note to his mother. Now he could get along without his allowance and could even give her a present of £300. The still lovely Jennie had recently married an officer no older than her son, and the couple's extravagant life often left them short of funds. "I could never have earned it had you not transmitted to me the wit and energy which are necessary," Winston told her.

He could now afford the life of a young man about town. He had a London flat. He traveled and played polo. He spent weekends as Sunny's guest at Blenheim. He was guest of the king at the royal hunting lodge in Scotland. Wherever he went it was always politics he wanted to talk about.

Four days after he took his seat in the House of Commons, he rose to make his maiden speech. The chamber and the visitors' gallery were crowded. Everyone was curious to see how "Randolph's boy" would acquit himself. He talked mostly about the war with the Boers, who continued to fight stubbornly on. He ended with a reference to his father. He said he knew the House had listened to him with "kindness and patience . . . because of a certain splendid memory which many honorable members still preserve."

There were speeches of congratulation. There was praise in the press. It was generally agreed that he had lived up to what people had expected of Lord Randolph's son.

Most new members of Parliament spoke seldom. Churchill spoke again within a few days, and regularly from then on. There was much he wanted to say.

He had never agreed with those Tories who thought the government's only task was the protection and expansion of the empire. In addition he thought the government should work for the principles of what his father had called Tory Democracy: peace, economy, and social reform. Not all his ideas had been inherited from his father, however; many of them were his own.

The need for social reform had suddenly seemed especially clear to him after he read a new book about poverty in English cities. He had not known such utter poverty existed anywhere in the world's most powerful nation. He had often thought of himself as pinched for money, but he had never known a day, he once admitted, when he couldn't afford a bottle of champagne for himself and another for a friend. The book had therefore shocked him deeply by showing him that thousands of English men, women, and children went to bed hungry every night. When Tory leaders wanted to tax imported grain and other raw materials, he said, "A tax on grain would raise the cost of bread for the poor."

Over and over again he rose in the House to urge its members to vote down bills his own party had proposed.

Tory leaders were soon complaining about him as they had once complained about his father. They said he was impudent and troublesome. They found him particularly irritating because they soon had to admit that he was becoming the best speaker in the House. Cartoonists drew pictures of "cheeky" Churchill, and comedians made jokes about him.

"You ain't 'alf got the cheek!" one popular comic said to another. "'Oo do yer think yer are? Winston Churchill?"

Churchill laughed at the jokes and admired the cartoons. Nothing silenced him. If the Tories did not change their ways, he thought, they would no longer deserve to rule the British Empire, as they had done now for close to a quarter of a century.

One day when he had been in the House about three years, he got to his feet to make one more of his prodding speeches. The Tory prime minister immediately rose from his place and left the chamber. Other Tories followed. Some jeered at Churchill before they left.

Afterward he was surrounded by members of the opposition Liberal party who had become his good friends. They had made social reform, the very thing Churchill pleaded for, the basis of their party platform.

"Why stay in a party that insults you as you were insulted today?" one of the Liberals demanded. "Why not come over to us?"

Churchill had been aware of his growing sympathy with the Liberals. There was, in fact, only one important way in which he still disagreed with them. They favored granting the home rule which Irish members of Parliament had long been demanding for their own island; Churchill did not. He believed that an Irish Parliament, which would be controlled by the land's Catholic majority, would not treat Ireland's Protestant minority fairly.

During the past year or more, however, Churchill had often reminded himself that, in his opinion, Tories treated the poor unfairly. Since much of Ireland's population was poor, he had thus had to ask himself if Irish Protestants might not prefer the rule of their Catholic neighbors to the rule of British Tories.

"With you making speeches for us," one of his Liberal friends was saying, "we might even win the coming election. And then we could really do something important about social reform. Think about it, Winston."

The next time Churchill entered the House, he paused at the head of the middle aisle. Shoulders hunched, as always, he looked at the Tory benches on his left and the Liberal benches on his right. He started forward. Suddenly he turned sharply to the right and sat down.

In the language of the House, he had "crossed the floor" to sit among the Liberals. In the eyes of Tories who had known him since his birth, he had "ratted" on his own party. Now they hated him as a traitor to everything they stood for.

The Liberals welcomed him with open arms. They made him one of their candidates for the big city of Manchester in the next election. Churchill flung himself into the campaign with untiring enthusiasm. He made speeches. He wrote articles. He shook hands. He made more speeches.

Two weeks before the election another of his books appeared. He had been devoting all his spare time to it for almost three years. It was *Lord Randolph Churchill*, a biography of his father.

The reaction of the public was all he could have hoped for. Critics hailed the book as "brilliant" and "masterly." They made it clear that Churchill could never again be dismissed as a mere journalist, turning out sensational books to further his own career. They said he would now have to be taken seriously as one of England's important writers.

Within ten days Churchill was being taken seriously as a political leader too. The election was a triumph for him and for the whole Liberal party. The Tories were swept out of office. The Liberals set up their own government, and Churchill was given the important post of undersecretary for the colonies.

In the months that followed he was almost single-handedly responsible for framing a new government for the finally defeated Boers. Many members of Parliament thought the Boers should be kept under strict control. Churchill, who had learned to admire the Boers' rugged independence, felt they should govern themselves within the empire.

The king congratulated Churchill on the new Boer constitution. The Liberal prime minister, now Churchill's political leader, invited him to join his cabinet. At thirty-three—even younger than his father had been when he achieved such a position—Churchill took his place among the small group of men who guided the destinies of the empire.

The membership of that particular Liberal cabinet remained almost constant for seven years. Known afterward as "the most glittering" cabinet of modern times, it made changes in the whole fabric of British life. Churchill had an important hand in those changes, while serving the cabinet in three roles, one after the other: as president of the board of trade, as home secretary, and finally as first lord of the admiralty.

While he was still president of the board of trade, in September 1908, he married Clementine Hozier, a penniless aristocrat and one of the most beautiful women in England. Fashionable London filled the church for the wedding. The street outside was crowded with workers who had come to think of Churchill as their champion.

"Good luck, Winston!" they shouted at him as he and the new young Mrs. Churchill drove off after the ceremony.

He had amazed his friends, who had decided that he would never marry. The friends of Clemmie, as he always called her, had also been surprised. She herself admitted later, "I had of course heard a great deal about him—nothing but ill." Now her mother was assuring people that her new son-in-law was "gentle and tender, affectionate to those he loves." She and Clemmie had both come to agree with one of Churchill's oldest friends, who said, "The first time you meet Winston you see all his faults. Then you spend the rest of your life discovering his virtues."

"I married and lived happily every afterward," Churchill once wrote. Clemmie was intelligent, well educated, witty, and charming, and a staunch believer in Liberal principles. She was the perfect wife for a rising young Liberal statesman.

Churchill, who had long taken for granted that he would marry only when he could support a wife, was proud he and Clemmie could move from an apartment into a home of their own about the time their first child was born.

"She is awfully strong & her little hands shut like a vice on one's finger," Churchill wrote of his tiny red-headed daughter, Diana, after taking charge of her bath one morning. "She looks vy beautiful & is greatly improving in shape & size." He had already made up his mind that his children would not remain shut away from their parents' sight in a distant nursery.

Ever since his first cabinet appointment, Churchill had been working with new gusto and pleasure. With another cabinet member, Welsh-born David Lloyd George, he devised welfare programs that seemed new and startling at the time. The programs did not fully satisfy most socialist-minded Labor party members, but they were far too socialistic for the old-line Tories. Churchill and Lloyd George, attacked from both sides, stubbornly pushed through one bill after another. They reduced a miner's working day to eight hours. They set up machinery for settling strikes. They opened government employment offices. They began work on a bill to give workers the benefits of unemployment insurance.

The Liberals' new welfare program cost a great deal of money. To pay for it they decided upon a daring "People's Budget." Nothing like it had ever been proposed in a land where taxes were collected only to provide for national defense and other traditional government activities.

This new budget was deliberately designed to redistribute the nation's wealth. It would take money away from the rich, in the form of high land taxes, and spend it on aid to the landless poor.

Owners of large estates were outraged. Most of them were peers who sat in the House of Lords. When the budget was presented for their approval, they vetoed it.

Churchill and his Liberal friends had expected what he once called "the evil, ugly veto of the Peers."

The Liberals had made up their minds that this time they would not accept it. They promptly presented to the peers a Parliament bill which would give the House of Commons, alone, the right to pass all money bills. The measure also stated that the Lords could veto any bill only twice; and that if the Commons then passed it a third time, it would become law.

Everyone knew the Lords would never pass the Parliament bill voluntarily. Forcing them to pass it would demand clever strategy and a long bitter fight. Churchill was both a good strategist and a tough fighter.

The Liberals knew they could not win without the aid of their king, now George V. They also knew he was unwilling to take their side against the peers. So they first had to show him their strength by dissolving Parliament and calling for new elections twice in one year. They won both elections. Then, knowing they had the support of Labor and Irish members of the House, they openly threatened their sovereign. If the king still refused to meet their demand, they said, they would call for still another election and this time their campaign cry would be "King and Peers against the People!"

The king could not permit himself to be presented as an enemy of the people. He agreed to do as they wanted: if necessary he would create hundreds of new peers, all favorable to the Parliament bill, who would outvote all the "old" peers in the House of Lords and pass any legislation the Liberals wanted.

The peers realized they were defeated. Before the king could "pack" their House with newly-titled members of the Liberal and Labor parties, they passed the Parliament bill.

With that one important vote the peers gave up most of their power. Dukes and earls would go on sitting in the House of Lords. They would still hold debates and cast votes on certain bills, but they would never again have anything to do with the finances of government. They would never again have any real control over the empire's business. The reins of power had passed into the hands of the elected members of the House of Commons.

Churchill and the other reform-minded members of the Liberal party had achieved a historic victory. As a result, they could now push forward their social reforms. Only one debt remained to be paid before they had a free hand. They had promised early home rule to the Irish members of Parliament, in return for Irish support during the struggle with the peers.

Churchill found himself traveling constantly, speaking in favor of the Irish Parliament he had opposed so often. It was not always a pleasant task. Once, as he arrived in the Irish city of Belfast, 10,000 angry Protestants surrounded his car. Clemmie was with him, as she often was. He sat helplessly beside her while fists pounded the car roof and voices shouted that he had betrayed Ireland's Protestants. On another occasion, in Parliament, an Irish Protestant hit him squarely on the nose with a heavy book.

Churchill's campaign for Irish home rule, however, and the prison reform program he started as home secretary, had to share his attention with a new concern. He had become convinced that Europe was on the brink of war and that England must prepare for it by strengthening her navy, the British Empire's traditional first line of defense.

To most Englishmen a twentieth-century European war was still unthinkable. They knew that France, England's enemy for so long in times past, and France's neighbor Belgium, were now allied to England by friendly treaty. The English could point out that Germany had always been England's friend, and that Germany's ruler, Kaiser Wilhelm II—he was Queen Victoria's grandson—had often shown his fondness for his English relatives.

Churchill had met the genial kaiser more than once and liked him. He was nevertheless deeply suspicious of Germany's intentions. He believed she was determined to expand her territory and her influence, partly because she was jealous of the large African territories recently taken over by England and France.

Proof of what Germany had in mind, Churchill said, was the large well-equipped army she had created and the navy she was rapidly building.

"We must improve our own navy," Churchill insisted, "or we shall lose our mastery of the seas. In a war that would be fatal. Sea lanes are our life lines," he reminded anyone who would listen. "They tie us to our colonies. They bring us the food our small island cannot grow for itself. If war comes, we must be ready!"

Churchill began to pry into naval affairs by studying statistics, by boarding naval vessels at every opportunity and questioning everyone from captain to coal heaver.

He was appalled at what he learned. He said the ships were too few and too old-fashioned. He said the men were underpaid and undertrained. He said changes must be made immediately in order to prepare the fleet for what might be its most severe test.

"Winston is looking for a war again," his enemies said, and reminded the public how eagerly he had once hurried from one battlefront to another.

Churchill angrily denied the charge. He insisted he had always worked steadily for peace, so long as the chance for peace existed.

As tensions rose in Europe, more and more government leaders came to agree with him that war might now be inevitable. They also accepted his judgment that if war did come, a powerful British navy was essential. Some of them realized, suddenly, that Churchill now probably knew more about the navy than any man in the country and that only he had the driving energy to transform it swiftly into a modern fighting force.

"Would you like to be first lord of the admiralty?" Prime Minister Herbert Asquith asked Churchill abruptly one day late in the year 1911. The admiralty was responsible for naval affairs.

"Indeed I would," Churchill assured him.

He went to work immediately. In the past he had always preached military economy. Now he was eager to spend whatever money was necessary to bring the navy up to the standards he had set for it in his own mind.

He had seamen's pay raised and their living conditions bettered. He had officers' training programs improved. He had vessels equipped with more powerful guns. He had new ships built that could travel faster because they ran on oil instead of coal. To guarantee their fuel supply Churchill pushed through the House of Commons an agreement to invest government funds in an oil company in Persia, the present-day Iran.

He bought the navy's first planes because he realized, before many did, that planes would be useful for coast defense. As soon as the first ones were delivered, he wanted to learn to fly them. They were small and fragile, like all early planes, and accidents were frequent. Churchill did not tell Clemmie about a crash he survived. Even so, he knew she was worried about him, and that worry was not good for her. She was still weak after the birth of a new baby. Reluctantly he gave up flying "for many months & perhaps for ever," as he wrote her.

"This," he went on, "is a gift—so stupidly am I made —wh costs me more than anything wh cd be bought with money. So I am vy glad to lay it at your feet, because I know it will rejoice & relieve your heart."

The pilots who had given him his instructions were not always comfortable flying with him—he took too many chances—but he delighted them with his deep interest in their machines. "What is this?" he would ask, his finger stabbing a bit of metal. "What does it do?"

Seamen too knew that Churchill cared about every aspect of their ships and their equipment. "Here comes Winston!" was always the cry when his stocky figure was sighted coming up a gangplank.

He enjoyed what he was doing. He couldn't deny that, at least not to Clemmie. Having seen more of

With his wife Clemmie at his side, the first lord of the admiralty inspects an early plane.

war than most of his fellowmen, he was deeply aware of its horrors. With Prime Minister Asquith and other British statesmen he tried earnestly to seek peaceful solutions to the problems posed by the German kaiser's ambitions. But if war did come, he could envision the great victories his navy might achieve because of the work he was pushing forward each day.

As the lovely warm summer of 1914 drifted by, war seemed each day more unavoidable. "Everything tends toward catastrophe & collapse," he wrote late in July to Clemmie, whom he had sent to the country with the children. "I am interested, geared up & happy," he went on honestly. "Is it not horrible to be built like that? The preparations have a hideous fascination for me. . . . Yet I wd do my best for peace, & nothing wd induce me wrongfully to strike the blow."

A few days after he wrote that letter, on August 2, Germany declared war on Russia. The next day the kaiser's army marched into France and Belgium, ignoring the British ultimatum declaring that England would defend her allies if they were invaded. At midnight of August 4, England declared war. At that same moment Churchill sent out his order to the fleet: "Commence hostilities with Germany."

He knew the ships and the men were ready. He knew their readiness had been his own doing. He was deeply and proudly satisfied with what he had done.

9. World War I

From the very first days of what would come to be known as World War I—though for years it was called simply The Great War—the British navy performed superbly.

It transported troops safely across the English Channel to beleaguered France and Belgium. It brought fighting men to England from her distant colonies. It protected the merchant ships on which England depended for vital food and other supplies.

Before many months had passed German ships no longer dared venture out of their home ports. Until Germany developed her deadly submarines later in the war, her navy remained largely helpless. The fleet Churchill had brought into being was in total command of the seas.

The fleet's tiny air force, the first Royal Navy Air Service, was also playing an important part in the war. It was responsible for defending England from Germany's great silver airships called Zeppelins. Churchill sent his flimsy little planes to Europe to raid the Zeppelin hangars inside Germany. They destroyed six of the huge airships within a year.

Churchill also sent to Europe a small group of

marines and the world's first armored cars—a number of London buses which he had had covered with heavy metal plates. One of the marines' first tasks was to reinforce the French coastal town of Dunkirk. Soon they were making forays in all directions, startling the Germans and sometimes convincing them that large British reinforcements had arrived.

The marines of the "Dunkirk Circus," as the unit was soon called, were a noisy, daring crew. Churchill couldn't resist joining their skylarking now and then. In spite of having grounded himself once, for Clemmie's sake, he now often flew to Paris, after a morning at his desk, and flew back home again in time for dinner. Several times on those flights he narrowly escaped death in crash landings. Several men flying with him were seriously injured. He never was.

When he realized that the Germans could halt his armored buses by digging ditches across the roads, he scribbled down some ideas for a vehicle that could ignore ditches. Then he turned the ideas over to experts and put them to work on it. Most people laughed at the result—a clumsy object that moved on caterpillar treads. But when army officers were finally persuaded to make use of it, they learned how valuable it could be. Churchill's ideas had produced the world's first armored tank.

During the early months of the war, while the British

navy was clearing the seas and guarding the air, England and her allies were faring very badly on the ground. Time after time their land forces fell back under German attack. In October the important Belgian city of Antwerp came under siege, and word was sent to London that it could not hold out for more than five days. Britain's secretary for war, Lord Kitchener, asked Churchill to fly to Antwerp to make his own judgment of the situation. Churchill took off immediately.

The prime minister, Herbert Asquith, was pleased with the result of Churchill's mission to Antwerp. He noted in his diary that "Winston succeeded in bucking up the Belgians who gave up their idea of retreat." A friend who saw Churchill in Antwerp reported that he "dominated the whole place—the King, Ministers, soldiers, sailors."

Churchill had "tasted blood," as he said afterward. He wired the prime minister that he wanted to stay where he was. He wished to resign from the admiralty, he said, and "undertake the command" of Antwerp.

The astounded prime minister wired back that the admiralty could not do without him. He wanted to add, but didn't because he was very fond of Churchill, that the two major-generals in charge of Antwerp might not wish to take orders from a man who had never risen above the rank of lieutenant.

Churchill's offer to leave the admiralty and to give

up his place, with Asquith and Kitchener, as one of the three men chiefly responsible for the grand strategy of the war, had made even his closest friends uneasy. "It was the choice of a romantic child," one friend wrote unhappily.

Churchill reluctantly returned to London, but once there he threw himself into plans for opening a new front against the enemy. He and his colleagues had decided to attack the Dardanelles, the narrow strait connecting the eastern Mediterranean with the Black Sea. After much discussion they agreed that it would have to be a purely naval attack, since no army forces could be spared to join it. Once that was settled, Churchill assumed the heavy task of carrying out the plan.

The result was total disaster. The naval attack failed. An army force, belatedly summoned, went ashore on the Gallipoli Peninsula and was slaughtered. More than 40,000 men were killed. Another 200,000 were injured.

Blame for the whole catastrophe fell on Churchill. The defeat gave his Tory enemies an opportunity for a vicious personal attack. They declared Churchill had forced his unwilling colleagues to accept his Dardanelles plan and thus brought about the tragedy.

Eventually a Parliamentary investigation would prove that the loss of lives and ships at Gallipoli was the fault of bungling commanders on the spot. Churchill

After Churchill left the cabinet in 1915, he asked for combat duty. He is seen here (center) at the front in France.

was completely exonerated. That investigation did not take place, however, for many months.

In the meantime Tories were loudly denouncing the Liberal government which had entrusted the admiralty to Winston Churchill. They demanded an election which would give an angry public the opportunity to oust the Liberals from power.

Prime Minister Asquith knew that a bitter election at this time would disrupt the nation. He offered the only possible alternative. He suggested that Liberals and Tories join in England's first coalition government —the kind of government, in fact, which Churchill himself had suggested at the beginning of the war when he thought it would help unite England against her foes.

The Tories agreed to Asquith's proposal, provided Winston Churchill was dropped from the cabinet. Asquith felt he had no choice. He accepted Churchill's resignation as first lord of the admiralty.

"I'm finished," Churchill told a friend. "I'm done."

Not many weeks later he was on his way to France, where he offered to take any command the military authorities might give him. His despairing mood was gone. Without the responsibility of a post, he felt free to seek the kind of action that one part of his nature always craved.

He assumed he would be given a brigade. He did

not complain when he was offered the smaller command of a battalion of Scots fusiliers. When he arrived at its headquarters, a bug-infested farmhouse, the Scots eyed him suspiciously. They could not understand why a famous English politician should suddenly appear as their commander.

Churchill called his staff together.

"Gentlemen," he announced, "war is declared—on the lice."

They stared at him unbelievingly. Was he joking, they wondered? They soon found he was not. First he gave them a long lecture on the habits and history of the tiny lice which every soldier found everywhere in the filthy mud of the battlefield—on his clothes, his blankets, himself. Then he ordered the men to strip and boil their clothes and blankets, and to scrub themselves. In three days his battalion was probably the only unit free of lice on the whole French front.

Although the men still laughed at Churchill when he took his own daily bath in a tin tub set up under a tree beside a blaring phonograph, they were beginning to be proud of what one Scots captain called "the wonderful genius of the man."

Churchill found brandy to serve at his staff dinners. He persuaded the men to sing at their work, and the Scots, never noted for their singing, looked amazed when they heard themselves joining in the songs

Churchill taught them. He never made his rounds of inspection in the safety of the trenches. Instead, in the blue tin helmet he had found somewhere, he walked above ground in constant danger from enemy fire. Shells fell close to him and exploded on spots he had left a moment before. None ever hit him.

Churchill lost his command only because the unit was broken up at the end of several months. He returned home looking as refreshed as if he had been on a vacation. He went promptly to the House of Commons and took what was now a lowly seat, far from the front benches where the government leaders sat.

By the time the parliamentary hearing on the Gallipoli disaster was over, and his name was cleared, his old friend Lloyd George had replaced the tiring Asquith as prime minister. Lloyd George and Churchill had become known, in their early days together in the Liberal party, as "the heavenly twins of Social Reform." Now Lloyd George, overcoming a weakened Tory resistance, named Churchill to his cabinet. Once more moving from post to post, Churchill remained in the cabinet until the war was over. He was minister of munitions. Next, and at the same time, he was secretary for war and secretary for air. Finally he was colonial secretary. Once again he was helping direct the course of the war and the fate of the empire.

At the war's end Churchill hoped for a settlement

that would be wisely generous toward the defeated enemy and thus lay the foundation for real peace. Lloyd George and many leaders of the Allies agreed with him, but the majority of the people they represented did not. "Punish the Germans!" they demanded. The harsh terms of the Versailles Treaty did that. It cost the Germans heavily in land and money, and deprived them of the right to arm. Churchill doubted that even the new League of Nations, weakened as it was by the failure of the United States to join it, could preserve the hard-won peace.

In the meantime another development had taken place that disturbed him deeply. The revolution that had broken out in Russia during the war had brought the Communists to power there, and Churchill regarded them as a major threat to the world.

He said "twenty or thirty thousand resolute, comprehending, well-armed Europeans" should be sent to Russia to destroy the Communists. War-weary Europeans could not be rallied to his crusade. Only his old colleagues, the Tories, seemed to share his strong feelings. Churchill formed an awkward alliance with them on that one subject. It persisted even after England officially recognized the new Soviet government.

Churchill was far more satisfied with other postwar developments in which he had a hand. He helped establish Irish home rule, plans for which had been abruptly dropped when the war began, and a national home for Jews in what was then called Palestine. He also helped bring into being new regimes friendly to England in other Mideast lands.

One day when the war had been over for about three years, Churchill drove through the lovely county of Kent, not far from London. His old nurse, Mrs. Everest, had been born there. She had filled his childhood with stories of Kent's profusion of "strawberries, cherries, raspberries and plums." He had always wanted to live in Kent. Thus, when he saw an old house surrounded by overgrown gardens and gnarled trees, he bought it immediately, using a sizeable legacy he had recently received from a distant relative. Chartwell Manor, as the house was called, would be the permanent Churchill home from then on.

The next year he had plenty of time to spend in Chartwell. That year the Tory party recaptured control of England's government. The end of the war, people had imagined, would mean days of golden plenty. Instead they had found themselves facing all the problems of a disturbed economy—labor unrest, unemployment, and strikes. So they had voted for the Tory party which promised to restore order and prosperity.

Churchill went down to defeat with his party. For the first time in twenty-one years he found himself without a seat in the House of Commons.

10. Warrior with a Pen

Churchill was restless in his new and unaccustomed leisure. A friend who saw him vacationing in France said he appeared to be waiting for a political call.

When the call did not come, Churchill plunged into the writing of a massive four-volume history of the war. Most critics admired it, but one political enemy said Churchill had written so much about himself that it was really "Winston's brilliant autobiography, disguised as the history of the universe."

Churchill had tried to make men understand that war in the twentieth century was so terrible a catastrophe that it must never be allowed to happen again.

"The Great War," he wrote, "differed from all ancient wars in the immense power of the combatants and their fearful agencies of destruction, and from all modern wars in the utter ruthlessness with which it was fought." He reminded his readers of the horror of bombs from the air and spoke of poison gas that had "stifled or seared" its victims. The weapons of any future war, he said, would be "incomparably more formidable and fatal," and could destroy all mankind.

As he wrote he had kept a constant watch on the

course of daily events. He had seen people turning against the Tory party for not fulfilling its promises. The voters did not simply turn back to the Liberals, however. Instead they were ready for what they hoped would be a completely new kind of regime. For the first time they voted into office the socialist-minded Labor party.

Many Liberals, realizing their own party could not win the election, had given the Labor party their support. Churchill was not among them. He could not bring himself to approve of Labor's socialist ideas. He announced that he now belonged to a new party, of which he was the only member. He called himself an antisocialist Constitutionalist, and under that label he ran for office in Westminster.

Westminster is the heart of London—a strange mixture of slums and mansions, of shabby theaters and magnificent state buildings. Westminster Abbey and the Houses of Parliament are in the district. So is Buckingham Palace. Among the people who rallied to the lone Constitutionalist were, Churchill recorded, "dukes, jockeys, prize-fighters, courtiers, actors and business men."

Titled ladies distributed leaflets in slum neighborhoods and invited the residents to tea. Chorus girls sat up all night addressing envelopes. Some of Churchill's oldest Tory colleagues, delighted that he no longer called himself a Liberal, joined in his fight—although, Churchill said, they "never liked or trusted me."

As the vote-counting neared its end on election night, his victory seemed certain.

"You're in!" someone shouted.

The cheer in the room was heard in the streets outside, and newsmen rushed to report Churchill's election to the public.

The report proved false. The final tally showed that Churchill had lost by forty votes.

Undaunted, he ran again under the same label at a special election five months later. On that occasion, with increased Tory aid, he won.

For the second time in his life, then, Churchill "crossed the floor" and returned to the Tory benches in the House of Commons. He was immediately named to the post his father had held at the peak of his career: he became chancellor of the exchequer.

Striding into the House not long afterward, he was gleefully aware that he had "ratted" his party twice —and that each time he had been rewarded with a post in the cabinet.

"You know," he once told a friend, "the family motto of Marlborough from whom I descend is 'Faithful but Unfortunate.' But I, by my enterprise, nay daring, have reversed the motto to 'Faithless but Fortunate.'"

The most dramatic event during his four and a half

Clemmie smiles her support as Winston campaigns
for a seat in Commons in 1924.

years as chancellor was a general strike that disrupted the whole country. Before it was settled he had taken over a struck newspaper plant and personally edited a paper he called *The British Gazette*. He was proud that it had a circulation of over two million copies on its eighth and last day of publication. He was not pleased when some people reminded him that his "strike-breaking" paper might owe its popularity to the fact that it was London's only paper that day.

On the floor of the House, at about the same time, Churchill was being abused by Tory colleagues. They were finally willing to grant India the self-government she was demanding. Churchill believed India would explode into civil war if her Hindu and Moslem populations were left to govern themselves. He was still as convinced as ever that British rule was wiser than any other.

His post of chancellor of the exchequer, or director of the national budget, often led to that of prime minister, the chief position in the government. But by now Churchill had been in politics long enough to understand why his opinionated father had never won that post, and why his own quarrel with Tory leaders might deprive him of it. He was not surprised when, in 1931, the coalition government, brought about by a worldwide financial crisis, made another man prime minister. His Tory enemies were so strongly opposed to Churchill that he was not even invited to join the cabinet.

"This time he is really ruined," people said. "And it is his own fault."

Looking suddenly old and ailing, Churchill retired to Chartwell Manor. When he went up to London to take his seat as an ordinary member of Parliament, his voice was seldom heard. Now he could not replace lost power with action on a battlefield. He had to content himself with an almost wholly domestic life— with Clemmie, his three daughters and his son, with his home, his writing, and his hobbies.

"Sitting in armchairs in front of the fire and going to sleep—that's what I'm getting used to," he muttered to a friend.

It was not possible for him to sit and do nothing for very long, however. Soon he was writing and selling articles. Then he collected the articles into books and sold them too.

He wrote *My Early Life*, a record of his boyhood and his adventures as a soldier and a young correspondent. This autobiography gave him a chance, at long last, to pay tribute to his old nurse, Mrs. Everest, whom he felt his family had neglected in her old age. He alone—he had been a Sandhurst cadet at the time —had hurried to her bedside when he heard she was poor and ill, and provided the care she needed. He said his awareness of her poverty, after a life of service to others, had helped turn his interest to the problems of social welfare.

My Early Life also gave him the chance to say something about the whipping of schoolboys, and the man who had taught him English. While other students were studying the Latin and Greek he could never master, he had remained in that teacher's class "three times as long as anyone else."

"Thus I got into my bones," he went on, "the essential structure of the ordinary British sentence—which is a noble thing. . . . Naturally I am biased in favor of boys learning English. I would make them all learn English: and then I would let the clever ones learn Latin as an honor, and Greek as a treat. But the only thing I would whip them for is for not knowing English. I would whip them hard for that."

His next book required vast research and the service of more than one hardworking secretary. It was a massive four-volume biography of the first duke of Marlborough.

When Churchill left his study it was often because he felt the urge to paint. He had begun painting some years earlier, when he had been dropped from the admiralty. He found it an utterly absorbing pastime. Shading his round bald head with a big white hat, and wearing a long white coat, he attacked a canvas as if it were his worst enemy. He used broad strokes of his brush and only the brightest colors. He wanted nothing to do with what he called the "poor browns." One day he would write a book about painting, urging other people to enjoy what he called "an unceasing voyage of entrancing discovery."

Other pastimes also kept him out of doors. He worked in the Chartwell garden. He dug a pool there with his children's help and devised an elaborate system for warming the water in it. He was especially proud of his skill at building brick walls. Members of the bricklayers union even complained that he was cheating them out of jobs. Churchill's reply was to earn membership in their union and regularly pay his union dues.

As the years went by, his voice was heard again in the House, first occasionally, then more frequently and more insistently. He had one subject: the threat of another war in Europe.

For a time he seemed almost alone in his belief that such a war could happen. His colleagues told him he was crying doom just to call attention to himself.

Adolph Hitler had risen to power in Germany, rearming a nation long embittered by the terms of the Versailles Treaty. In 1936 Hitler seized territory along the Rhine River which that treaty had denied to Germany. At the same time another new dictator, Italy's Mussolini, invaded Abyssinia in North Africa.

Churchill returns to the familiar office of the first
lord of the admiralty to help plan Britain's defenses
in World War II.

Churchill demanded that the other nations of Europe —the members of the League of Nations—take a firm stand against the aggressive moves of those two men. To do so effectively, he added, these countries must build up their own strength. He also pointed out that England's defenses had fallen into a state of "lamentable weakness and confusion." Only a strong and united stand, he insisted, could put an end to the "hideous drift of events."

"Stop it! Stop it! Stop it now!!!" he wrote. "NOW is the time."

Gradually men came to heed his warnings, but when they did, events were no longer drifting. They were moving swiftly. In March of 1939 Hitler's Nazi forces seized part of Czechoslovakia. The following month Mussolini's Fascists invaded Albania. Then suddenly all seemed quiet. French and English leaders hoped that the dictators' greed had been satisfied, and that war could after all be avoided.

They had miscalculated. Hitler invaded Poland on September 1, 1939. This time England and France took the step Churchill had been saying they must take eventually. They declared war on Germany.

That same day, September 3, Churchill was called back into a Conservative government which had kept him out of its councils and ignored his advice for so long. He became once more the first lord of the admiralty. Instantly a signal went out to all ships with a message that brought cheer to hundreds of seamen. The message read simply, "Winston is back!"

During the next six months the British navy won a decisive victory over the German fleet, but Germany's land forces were everywhere victorious. The Germans had already seized Norway when, on May 10, 1940, they marched simultaneously into Belgium, the Netherlands, and Luxembourg. They were on their way to France. From France, they made it clear, they would launch the invasion Hitler had promised his people— the invasion of England.

The Conservative prime minister, Neville Chamberlain, resigned. His efforts toward peace had earlier won him public praise, but now he was being widely blamed for having appeased Hitler too long. It was clear, not only to Churchill but to many others, that at this moment only a coalition government, combining the leadership of Britain's three parties, could express the population's will to fight and guide the nation. Chamberlain would not be acceptable as the leader of such a coalition. King George sent for Churchill, who had confidently expected the summons.

For weeks he had seen posters in the streets hailing him as the man who had been right all along. "Churchill Must Come Back!" the posters demanded.

The still youthful king look quizzically at the man

he had known all his life, and who had served his brother Edward VIII before him, and his father and grandfather before that. "I suppose you don't know why I have sent for you," he said.

Churchill answered in the same carefully light tone. "Sir, I simply couldn't imagine why," he said.

"I want you to form a government," the king told him.

"I will certainly do so, sir," Churchill assured him.

He was prime minister at last, at the age of sixty-five —not as vindication of his father, but as vindication of his own long career of devotion to what he saw as the best interests of the British Empire. Had he died a year earlier, at an age when many men die, he would have gone down in history, one Englishman pointed out, as "a brilliant failure, a politician without a party, without power, without influence." He had not died.

"I was kept for this job," Churchill once told a friend.

He went to bed that night, he later wrote, with "a profound sense of relief. . . . I felt as if I were walking with Destiny, and that all my past life had been but a preparation for this hour and this trial. . . . I could not be reproached either for making the war or with want of preparation for it. I thought I knew a good deal about it all, and I was sure I should not fail. Therefore, although impatient for the morning, I slept soundly and had no need for cheering dreams. Facts are better than dreams."

11. Prime Minister

The following Monday, May 13, 1940, Winston Churchill addressed the House of Commons for the first time as prime minister.

"I have nothing to offer but blood, toil, tears, and sweat," he said.

"You ask, what is our policy?" he went on. "I will say: It is to wage war, by sea, land, and air, with all our might and with all the strength that God can give us: to wage war against a monstrous tyranny. . . . You ask, what is our aim? I can answer in one word: Victory—victory at all costs, victory in spite of all terror, however long and hard the road may be. . . ."

Churchill's colleagues in Parliament, indeed the entire British public, felt he was expressing precisely their own thoughts and their own determination.

Early on the second morning after that speech, Churchill was awakened by a telephone call from France, where British soldiers were fighting beside French, Dutch, and Belgian forces.

"We have been defeated," French Premier Paul Reynaud told him.

Churchill took for granted he was being told of

the loss of a battle. Calmly he reminded Reynaud that many defeats might precede a final victory and said he would fly to Paris the next day to discuss plans.

By the time he reached Paris, terrified families were fleeing the city, and government clerks were burning secret files. The Germans were expected within a few days. A cease-fire had already been proclaimed in the Netherlands.

Still thinking of how best to launch an offensive against the oncoming enemy, Churchill questioned the French general commanding both French and British forces. "Where is your strategic reserve?"

"There is none," the general said.

Dumbfounded that the commander had left himself without reserves, Churchill wired his war cabinet for more British fighter planes, although it meant reducing Britain's own defenses to a minimum.

Nothing stemmed the German tide. Hour by hour it drove the Allied armies ahead of it across France toward the English Channel.

Churchill suggested a union of France and England. He said it would permit France to fight on from her colonies or from England if need be, should her homeland be overrun. The French leaders refused. Such a union would be useless, one leader explained, because "in three weeks England will have her neck wrung like a chicken."

Churchill felt that there was only one thing left to do. He summoned an armada for a rescue mission. Hundreds of English vessels responded, large and small —some naval destroyers and gunboats, many privately owned craft ranging from coal freighters and luxury yachts to little outboard motorboats. Night after night they all plowed back and forth across the treacherous Channel, risking enemy mines below and enemy aircraft overhead. They brought to England thousands of exhausted English and French soldiers who had gathered on the beaches at Dunkirk, the sole stretch of the French northern coast not yet in enemy hands. Vast amounts of valuable military equipment had to be left behind, but the evacuation of Dunkirk would always remain one of the most gallant chapters in British history.

By the time that chapter ended, France lay stricken. From then until almost the end of the war Germans occupied Paris and a large part of French territory. The rest of the country was governed by those French authorities, headquartered in Vichy, who had submitted to the Nazis' terms of surrender.

Will England surrender too? the world was asking. Hitler's answer was that it must.

Churchill's answer was a radio address to his fellow Englishmen. "We have become the sole champions in arms to defend the world cause," he said. "We shall do our best to be worthy of this high honor."

To his cabinet he said privately, "Well, gentlemen, we are alone. For myself, I find it extremely exhilarating."

His first concern was to prevent the powerful French fleet from falling into the hands of the Nazis, who could use it to destroy supply lines from Britain's empire and the United States. Those ships that happened to be in British ports when France surrendered were easily taken over. The large French naval force in the Mediterranean was a different problem. Churchill offered its admiral several choices: to join the British; to sail his ships to a distant American or Caribbean port where they would be safe from the Germans; or to scuttle his fleet. If he accepted none of them, Churchill said, the British navy would be forced to attack the vessels. When the French admiral did refuse them all, Churchill was true to his word: he ordered the British Mediterranean fleet to attack. Only one French ship escaped; the rest were effectively put out of action.

Many Englishmen were horrified at such drastic action against their "dearest friends of yesterday." Churchill insisted it had been necessary. He added grimly that it proved to the world "that the British war cabinet fears nothing and would stop at nothing."

Now began the blitz, the long and bitter Battle of Britain. German bombers and fighter planes had been ordered to destroy the Royal Air Force, Britain's chief defense against invasion. They first engaged British airmen over the Channel and the Channel ports. When that did not result in England's surrender, the German aircraft flew farther inland, seeking out airdromes, aircraft production centers, and the nation's largest cities. The Germans suffered severe losses from British defenders, but there seemed always to be new German planes to replace those that were shot down.

By early September the enemy was regularly bombing London. Every evening, shortly after dusk, as many as 200 planes reached the ancient capital and dropped their bombs. Whole blocks collapsed into rubble. Each morning brought to 10 Downing Street, the prime minister's official residence, its new toll of death and destruction, its latest report of imminent invasion.

Churchill read the reports in bed, where he worked each morning after a night spent in an air raid shelter deep underground. There he read the memos which arrived in the prime minister's special dispatch case, always called his "box"—memos which he insisted should never be more than a page or two long. There he dictated the notes and letters that went out from 10 Downing Street in a steady stream, many of them demanding, in his peremptory phrase, "Action This Day."

Later he lunched with advisers and then returned to bed for the brief sleep which permitted him to go

Although there must have been many times when Churchill felt the heavy burden of responsibility, he gave strength and courage to his countrymen whose homes and businesses had been bombed.

on working long after midnight, to the exhaustion of many of his aides who were years younger than he was. He liked to tell friends that he had learned the value of an afternoon nap, or siesta, when he was getting his first taste of war in Cuba.

Once a week, on Tuesday, he lunched with the king and queen at bomb-damaged Buckingham Palace. No servants waited on the elderly prime minister and his sovereigns. They served themselves and carried their own plates and glasses down to the palace shelter when a raid occurred.

Churchill kept the king fully informed of what was happening, not only throughout England but in the Mediterranean, for example, where British ships were fighting, and in North Africa where British soldiers were battling an Italian attack on Egypt. These were the same problems Churchill regularly discussed with his war cabinet.

The problems seemed infinite in number and variety. They included the speeding up of aircraft and armament production; the food rationing demanded by reduced imports; the source of a safe water supply if London's water mains were destroyed; the possibility of a glass "famine" brought on by the shattering of thousands of windows; the best equipment for the volunteer fire-watchers who stationed themselves on London's roofs each night to spot and put out the blazes set by incendiary bombs; the best training for the special squads assigned to defusing delayed-action bombs; instructions for the million and a half home guards who stood ready to fight invaders, as Churchill said, "for every inch of the ground in every village and every street."

Churchill also took the British people into his confidence by radio. He knew the listening nation shared his admiration for the British fliers who took to the air against the seemingly endless enemy squadrons. "Never in the field of human conflict was so much owed by so many to so few," he said of that handful of young men.

One September evening he was able to say, "Herr Hitler is using up his fighter force at a very high rate." He had to add, however, that Germany might invade the island within a week. Thus the days just ahead, he said, ranked "with the days when the Spanish Armada was approaching the Channel." He reminded his unseen audience of what they had all read in their history books about Sir Francis Drake leading the British fleet out to destroy the Spaniards. Now all Englishmen, he said, must take courage from the knowledge that they were living a moment of history of even more consequence to mankind.

The week passed. The invasion did not take place. Neither did the bombings cease. For fifty-seven consecutive nights bombs fell on London. The city of Coventry suffered the single most devastating blitz of the war. Birmingham was bombed, and Bristol, and Southampton, and Liverpool.

Churchill visited scene after scene of devastation, often with Clemmie at his side. A fat cigar was always clamped at an angle in his heavily jowled, bulldog-like face. Sometimes he was wearing the "siren suit" he had designed. It was a zippered overall that he could pull on in an instant when the screaming siren of a raid warning drove him from bed to shelter. His greeting to the crowds that gathered around him was the two raised fingers spread in a V, which all England had come to recognize as the sign of victory.

Everywhere he went people cheered him. Their spirit gave him strength. His nation, he boasted, "was as sound as the sea is salt."

One man outside of England in whom Churchill regularly confided was Franklin Delano Roosevelt, president of the United States. The two men did not know each other. Their relationship, based on each man's admiration for the other's qualities of leadership, was enriched by their mutual interest in naval affairs. Roosevelt had been an assistant secretary of the United States Navy before World War I, when Churchill first served as first lord of the admiralty.

Churchill rejoiced in Roosevelt's unprecedented election to a third term of office during the darkest days of the London blitz. Convinced that the United States would someday enter the war on Britain's side, Churchill felt sure Roosevelt shared his belief. The president's sympathy for Britain's cause had already been proved by his efforts to see that she obtained some of the ships and arms she so badly needed. Churchill realized, however, that American entry into the war might be long delayed. He himself had had to argue for years before most Englishmen agreed with him that a stand must be taken against Hitler's aggression. Roosevelt, he knew, might have even more difficulty swaying the opinion of his larger country separated from Europe's struggle by the width of the Atlantic.

In March of 1941 Churchill could nevertheless announce the cheering news of Lend-Lease. This plan, contrived by Roosevelt, permitted the United States to lend or to lease American-built equipment to Great Britain without payment from the British treasury, already strained by war to the breaking point. "Give us the tools," Churchill had promised Americans, "and we will finish the job."

Other news that spring was less cheering. German U-boats were causing serious damage to British shipping. The British island of Malta in the Mediterranean was under constant attack. British forces in North Africa fell back under the brilliant onslaught of German General

Erwin Rommel. Greece surrendered to the enemy, and not all the British forces that had been sent there could be evacuated.

On the night of May 10 more than 2,000 fires lit by incendiary bombs blazed in London alone. Over 3,000 people were killed or injured in the city that night, and a single bomb destroyed the House of Commons, citadel of British democracy. Standing in the smoking ruins of the building that had meant more to him than any other structure in the world, Churchill swore that it would be rebuilt, stone by stone, to its ancient pattern. Then he set about the mundane task of finding temporary quarters for the members of the House.

On the morning of June 22 Churchill's secretary woke him with information he had been expecting to receive for some days: Germany had invaded Russia. "I will broadcast at nine tonight," Churchill said.

He knew exactly what he wanted to say. He had done his best to prevent the success of the Russian revolution of 1917 that had brought Lenin to the seat of power which Joseph Stalin now occupied. Stalin had signed a nonaggression pact with Hitler in August of 1940, when many people had hoped he would ally himself instead with a Britain recently left alone to face its foe. Thus, Churchill knew, many people now expected him to express the hope that the communist nation would be destroyed—might even expect him to

The prime minister sadly surveys the ruins of the House of Commons.

suggest that Britain come to terms with Hitler, to assure that destruction.

Instead Churchill told the world that night that although he would "unsay no word" he had spoken against Communism in the past, he now felt that past had "flashed away."

"Can you doubt what our policy will be?" he demanded. "We have but one aim. . . . We are resolved to destroy Hitler and every vestige of the Nazi regime. From this nothing will turn us—nothing. . . . It follows therefore that we shall give whatever help we can to Russia and the Russian people."

He knew such help would have to be great. The German assault on the lengthy Soviet border was massive and powerful. Russia's entry into the war would therefore, perhaps for as long as a year, add a new burden to the ones England already carried. The attack nevertheless guaranteed, at least for a time, that Germany would not invade England—although that invasion would certainly take place if Hitler defeated the Soviet Union.

Some six weeks later Churchill was enjoying a pleasure he had long promised himself: he was talking face-to-face with Roosevelt. Under cover of secrecy he had crossed a rough Atlantic in the battleship *Prince of Wales*, with an escort of destroyers. With equal secrecy Roosevelt had made his way to Newfoundland. There the two met and instantly formed what Churchill described as "a dear and cherished friendship." "It is fun to be in the same century with you," Roosevelt one day told him. Churchill might have used the same words to the American president.

They discussed aid to Britain. They discussed aid to Russia and sent a joint message to Stalin assuring him of their support and suggesting an early meeting with him. They talked of the fighting that lay ahead and of the world they hoped for when the war ended with Hitler's defeat, as they were both totally convinced it must.

At Roosevelt's suggestion Churchill outlined a declaration of joint Anglo-American principles. Together they elaborated that outline into what would come to be known as the Atlantic Charter. It stated that neither country desired new territory, that both respected the right of all peoples to chose their own government, and that each sought a peace that would be assured "by effective international organization." Out of that charter would soon grow the United Nations. The two men hoped that this organization would do what the League of Nations had failed in the past to do: guarantee a world of peace and freedom for all mankind. The charter suggested that England and the United States together would police the world and prevent aggressive nations from obtaining arms until that organization of "general

Copyright, Karsh, Ottawa

Churchill exhibited fierce determination as he led his people through the perils of war.

security" was established to take over those functions. It was a document, Churchill wrote, of "profound and far-reaching importance."

He sailed home with renewed strength for the dark days he knew still lay ahead.

On the Sunday evening of December 7, 1941, less than four months later, Churchill turned on his radio a few moments late for the nine o'clock news report. The voice he heard was saying something about a Japanese attack on Americans. Churchill sat up, instantly alert. His valet came in at that moment and said the servants had heard on their own radio that there had been a Japanese naval attack on the American fleet in the Pacific.

Churchill put in an immediate call to the White House. Roosevelt was on the line within a few minutes.

"Mr. President, what's this about Japan?" Churchill asked.

"It's quite true," Roosevelt answered. "They have attacked us at Pearl Harbor. We are all in the same boat now."

Churchill did not learn, because Roosevelt himself did not yet know, that the American fleet had been almost completely destroyed. He could not guess that Japan would soon be in total control of the Pacific and Indian oceans, that even the British bastions of Hong Kong and Singapore would be in Japanese hands.

Churchill's first reaction was one of enormous relief.

"No American will think it wrong of me if I proclaim that to have the United States at our side was to me the greatest joy," he wrote later. He could admit now that until this moment Britain's eventual defeat had always been a possibility, even to him. Now he no longer had any doubts as to how the war would end. "United we could subdue everybody else in the world," he wrote.

He left within days for another dangerous crossing of the U-boat-infested Atlantic. At the insistence of his cabinet, a doctor traveled with him. He was in Washington by December 22. On Christmas Eve he stood with Roosevelt beside the traditional Christmas tree set up on the White House lawn and told the crowd gathered around it how much at home he felt in his mother's country.

The day after Christmas he addressed the joint Houses of Congress. It seemed to him that he was uniquely fitted to extend the hand of Britain to her powerful new ally.

"I cannot help reflecting that if my father had been American and my mother British, instead of the other way around, I might have got here on my own," he said.

The congressmen laughed, as he had wanted them to. From then on he was in deadly earnest. When speaking of their common enemy, the Japanese, he demanded,

"What sort of people do they think we are?" and the entire Congress rose to cheer him.

One night, in a White House bedroom that seemed too warm, he got up to open a window. He found it stiff to move. The strain brought on a pain in his chest. His doctor, the next morning, felt certain Churchill's heart had been at least slightly damaged. He also felt that to tell him—or the world—the truth at that moment in history would be disastrous. He kept silent, but from then on he did his best to persuade an always impatient Churchill to exert himself no more than necessary.

After a week's rest in the Florida sun, Churchill returned to England on January 17, 1942. A new year had begun—a year in which, as he would later write, "for the first six months . . . all went ill; for the last six months everything went well."

12. "Power to Shape the Future"

Churchill now faced the first serious criticism of his leadership. People were no longer closely united by an immediate threat of invasion. As they read reports of British defeats in other parts of the world, some blamed them on Churchill who had insisted upon serving as his own minister of defense. They said a new defense minister should be named to direct the war.

Churchill admitted freely that "things have gone badly," but he felt the troubles still ahead could be overcome only if, as he put it, "the prime and direct responsibility" for the war remained in his own hands. He "found it difficult to understand and impossible to forgive," a friend wrote later, "any patriotic and decent-minded Englishman" who criticized his policy. Instead of resigning as defense minister, Churchill demanded a vote of confidence. After three days of debate in the House he was given it, with only one vote cast against him.

In the months that followed there were new defeats by German forces in Africa, heavy losses to German U-boats in the Atlantic, and advances in the Pacific that brought Japanese forces close to India. Many

Indian leaders wanted to declare their territory independent of the British Empire, so that India could become neutral and thus spare herself a possible Japanese invasion.

Churchill could not readily agree to the loss of India. Reluctantly he approved a promise of Indian independence after the war, in return for full support during the fighting. Gandhi and other Hindu leaders were not satisfied with that promise, and the anti-British feeling they represented continued to plague Churchill. He was irritated when Roosevelt expressed his opinion that India had the right to immediate self-government.

"I have not become the King's First Minister in order to preside over the liquidation of the British Empire," Churchill announced brusquely. The statement made many Americans uneasy. They said it sounded like an echo of the nineteenth century. Churchill muttered that the president's mind was "back in the American War of Independence."

He was grateful for the president's sympathetic understanding, however, when in June some 30,000 British soldiers surrendered their arms to the enemy at the North African town of Tobruk. Churchill was again in Washington when he received the news. The telegram was handed to him by Roosevelt himself. At first Churchill could not believe the words he read. Then he felt disgraced before his American friends.

Roosevelt said only, "What can we do to help?"

Minutes later plans were being made to ship 300 American-built tanks to Africa. Churchill never forgot the generous offer, made at a time when American production was straining to supply the rapidly growing American forces.

The British surrender at Tobruk led to another attempt to unseat Churchill as minister of war. Once again he called for a vote of confidence and once again he won it—but this time twenty-five members of Parliament voted against him.

Russia's fierce struggle against German invaders had now lasted for many months, and she was insisting that her allies launch an attack which would draw off some of the Nazi strength. Stalin wanted that attack to be made in Europe. Churchill felt strongly that American recruits should not be used for such a difficult task until they had been seasoned in battle and that a European invasion which failed would be worse than none at all. He and the Americans finally agreed that the wisest first use of the new Anglo-American force should be in North Africa, where it was hoped it could destroy the enemy there. To explain the decision directly to Stalin, Churchill and his staff flew to Moscow in August.

At seven o'clock on the night of their arrival Churchill met the revolutionary warrior and statesman whom he had regarded, before the rise of Hitler, as mankind's most dangerous enemy. Stalin looked "very glum" when he heard that his allies would not launch a second front in Europe in 1942. He argued against a North African invasion. Then, Churchill reported, the Soviet leader "saw it all in a flash" and showed "swift and complete mastery of the situation."

At the end of Churchill's five-day visit, he sat over the dinner table with Stalin until two-thirty in the morning. They had established a relationship which for the next three years, Churchill once wrote, would be "intimate, rigorous, but always exciting, and at times even genial."

The Anglo-American landing in Africa, following a decisive British victory there at Alamein, took place in the fall. By January of 1943 Churchill and Roosevelt could meet in Casablanca, which had not long before been in German hands, to plan future strategy.

The two men were again together in May, in Washington, when Churchill received a message saying, "All enemy resistance has ceased. We are masters of the North African shores." The victorious Allies had taken a quarter of a million prisoners. They had opened the Mediterranean to Allied shipping for the first time since 1941.

This triumph almost wiped out for Churchill the grim memory of reading that message about Tobruk before

Churchill flashes the victory sign to seamen on the
ship that took him to the United States.

Roosevelt's sympathetic eyes. As he drove with the president and his wife to their Maryland mountain retreat, he asked to be shown the home of the Civil War heroine Barbara Frietchie. He had learned Whittier's poem about her when he was a boy. His American hosts knew only its two most famous lines:

> "Shoot if you must this old gray head,
> But spare your country's flag," she said.

Churchill smugly recited it all the way through. Both he and Roosevelt much preferred talking to listening. This was one occasion when the president did not dare to interrupt him.

In July of 1943 the Allied forces invaded and took over the control of Sicily and then landed on the Italian mainland to begin the long stubborn fight up the boot-shaped peninsula. Italians arrested Mussolini and sought an armistice through their new government. In October Italy officially declared war on her one-time friend, Germany, who now used Italy as a battlefield for some of the bloodiest fighting of the war.

In November Churchill was in Cairo, eating the Thanksgiving turkey which Roosevelt had brought along to their conference there. Roosevelt's son Elliott was with him as his aide. Since Churchill's son Randolph was serving with the British forces, usually one of his daughters accompanied him on his travels. Sarah was her father's aide this time. Afterward Churchill and Roosevelt went on to the Iranian city of Teheran, for their first joint meeting with Stalin.

During that session, crowded with lengthy discussions of war strategy, Churchill marked his sixty-ninth birthday with a dinner at which Roosevelt sat on his right and Stalin on his left. He enjoyed the evening both as a host and as a historian. Three such powerful men, he felt sure, had never before gathered around a dinner table.

"Together," he wrote later, "we controlled practically all the naval and three-quarters of all the air forces in the world, and could direct armies of nearly twenty millions of men."

In one of the toasts proposed after dinner, an American said he had long studied the unwritten British constitution and had decided that its provisions "are just whatever Winston Churchill wants them to be at any given moment."

Churchill laughed with the others. Then he said, "But I must remind you that I am the only one of our trinity who could at any moment be dismissed from power. You can order. I must convince and persuade. And I am glad that this is so," he insisted. "It is a laborious process, but I have no reason to complain of the way it works."

By the following January, having recovered from his second bout of pneumonia in less than a year, Churchill was presiding at weekly conferences on the proposed Allied invasion of France—the "second front" which Stalin had so long sought. It was to take place in June, under the command of the American General Dwight D. Eisenhower.

As the date of D-day, or landing day, drew near, Churchill made plans to be on one of the cruisers that would approach the French coast. Eisenhower, concerned for his safety, urged him to change his mind. Churchill refused. Then the king, who would have liked to accompany him, said he felt neither of them should go.

Churchill remained determined. A man making "grave and terrible decisions of war may need the refreshment of adventure," he explained. "He may need also the comfort that when sending so many others to their death he may share in a small way their risks." He was on the train heading for the cruiser's port when the king made an appeal he couldn't refuse.

"I am a younger man than you," the king wrote. "I am a sailor, and as King I am the head of all these Services. There is nothing I would like better than to go to sea, but I have agreed to stay at home; is it fair that you should then do exactly what I should have liked to do myself?"

Sadly Churchill returned to London, after only a brief visit to General Eisenhower's headquarters from which the launching of the invasion was to take place.

D-day had been scheduled for June 5. Bad weather forced a postponement for twenty-four hours. Then 4,000 ships, the greatest armada ever to leave England's shores, set out on a rough sea. Rome had fallen to the Allies two days earlier. Soviet soldiers were about to launch a new offensive against the invaders of their land. The first serious defeats had been inflicted on the Japanese. All omens for the success of the great new venture seemed excellent.

The landing, supported by airborne divisions parachuted into France, was a total surprise to the enemy. By the afternoon of D-day Churchill could report to Stalin, "Everything has started well. The mines, obstacles, and land batteries have been largely overcome. The air landings were very successful, and on a large scale. Infantry landings are proceeding rapidly, and many tanks and self-propelled guns are already ashore . . ."

Four days later Churchill could visit the British commander in his headquarters in a French chateau five miles inland from the landing beaches.

On the night of June 12, the first German flying bombs exploded on London. These buzz bombs, as the British named them from the sound of their engines, could travel 400 miles an hour and each carried a ton of explosives. They were too fast and too small to be intercepted by planes. During the next several months London and the countryside around it suffered severely. Some three-quarters of a million houses were damaged; twenty-three thousand of them were totally destroyed.

In September came still another new German weapon, the V-2 rocket. Speeding silently through the skies, it gave no warning of its approach. In seven months, before its launching site in Belgium could be destroyed, it caused nearly 3,000 deaths in England and more than 6,000 other casualties.

Churchill was convinced, however, that even these destructive weapons could only postpone Germany's defeat; they could not prevent it. A ring of Allied armies, including forces that had landed on the south coast of France, were now closing inexorably around the foe. Before the end of August Paris was liberated and its joyful citizens flooded the streets, embracing their rescuers. As the Germans were pushed back toward their homeland they fought more desperately than ever. By this time Churchill knew that even some German leaders must realize the end was inevitable.

His own chief concern had become the settlement that would follow the victory of what he called the Grand Alliance, especially in view of "the upsurge of Communist influence" in the world. He had had agreeable talks with Stalin, but his mistrust of the Soviet Union was as strong as ever. He was troubled because

At their Yalta Conference—the Big Three of World
War II: Churchill, Roosevelt, and Stalin

he thought the United States was, as he put it, "very
slow in realizing" the strength of that upsurge.

He believed, as he always had, that the democracies
"could only reach good decisions with Russia while we
had the comradeship of a common foe as a bond."
Together the three powers were destroying that foe.
"But after Hitler what?" Churchill demanded. He felt
sure he saw the answer more clearly than Roosevelt did.
"Communism," he wrote, "would be the peril civilization
would have to face."

At what would be his final meeting with Roosevelt

and Stalin, at Yalta in the Russian Crimea in February 1945, Churchill toasted Stalin at their last dinner as a friend.

There were sharp exchanges during their conference, however, as they tried to lay the groundwork for the new European governments that would come into existence at the war's end. The exchanges were equally sharp as they tried to establish a working framework for the United Nations, soon to hold its first meeting.

Some weeks later, in April, Churchill proved how little he really trusted Stalin by urging Eisenhower to hasten the movement of his forces. He wanted them to "shake hands with the Russians as far to the east as possible." He was convinced the Russians would lay claim to any territory they captured as they moved westward to meet the eastward-moving Anglo-American armies.

The meeting of those armies brought about Germany's unconditional surrender on May 7. Churchill broadcast the news to his people. It was the signal, he wrote, "for the greatest outburst of joy in the history of mankind."

He had achieved the goal he had set himself when he became prime minister: Hitler had been destroyed. Churchill's own joy, however, was overshadowed by his sorrow at Roosevelt's sudden death a few weeks before and by his concern for the future.

"There is still a lot to do," he warned his countrymen. "We must make sure that those causes which we fought for find recognition at the peace table." He hoped the United Nations would prove equal to its purpose.

His responsibility to solve the problems of peace seemed even heavier to him now that Roosevelt was gone. He hoped to have the support of his coalition government until solutions were reached along the lines he and Roosevelt had agreed upon. That government had been in power for almost five years, however, and British law demanded an election. Churchill suggested a referendum that could maintain the coalition at least until Japan was defeated. Leaders of the Labor party said their members would not agree to that.

British trade-union members had been dreaming of a "brave new world" in which they would enjoy the kind of prosperity they felt the hard-won victory entitled them to. The Labor party had been drawing up plans for such a world. Its members insisted upon the opportunity to vote it into power.

Churchill resented the need to distract his attention from world affairs to British politics. He campaigned impatiently before the election, which took place July 5. Before its results were known—they would not be announced until July 26, to permit the counting of votes from distant military posts—he went to Potsdam, in Germany, for another meeting of the Big Three. Stalin was present and, for the first time, President Harry S. Truman represented the United States.

In Potsdam, Churchill and Truman learned of the successful testing of the first atomic bomb. Churchill was in instant agreement with Truman to use the bomb against Japan. It would bring a quick end to the war, he thought, with "one or two violent shocks." It would save "a million American lives and half that number of British—or more, if we could get them there: for we were resolved to share the agony." It would also mean that "we should not need the Russians," who had promised to enter the Japanese war as soon as possible. The Russians would therefore have no opportunity to extend their power into the Pacific.

Churchill, King George, and the royal family greet the English people after the victory in Europe. The present queen, Elizabeth, is at the left.

Stalin was told several days later that the United States had developed a new and unusual bomb, but he was given no particulars that would suggest its true significance to the war effort.

Churchill and his daughter Mary flew home from Germany on July 25 to hear the election results in England. That night they had a quiet family dinner with Clemmie.

"I hear the women are for me," Churchill had said to Clemmie once, when they were talking of the election.

Clemmie knew his heart had not been in his campaign broadcasts. She knew he seemed no longer able to speak for the people, now that their minds were so attuned to thoughts of domestic peace and prosperity. However, she only reminded him of how bitterly he had once opposed votes for women during his early days in Parliament.

"Quite true," Churchill agreed, but he went to bed confident that the nation still demanded his leadership.

By noon the next day the results were in: Labor had won overwhelmingly.

Churchill had pointed out to Roosevelt and Stalin at his birthday dinner in Teheran that he could be dismissed from power at any moment. He had not really thought it would happen. He was stunned. Was this the way England thanked him, he wondered, for leading her to victory?

Clemmie, knowing better than he did how weary her seventy-year-old husband was, said calmly, "This may well be a blessing in disguise."

"If so, it seems quite effectively disguised!" Churchill retorted.

His defeat meant to him that "the power to shape the future would be denied me." That future was now at hand. On August 14, after two atomic bombs had been dropped on Japan, killing more than 100,000 people, Japan surrendered. Her fate and the fate of Europe were now to be directed by the leaders of the victorious nations. Churchill was no longer one of these men. He was the leader now of only the broken and defeated Tory party.

13. "I Had the Luck..."

Churchill's doctor had been urging him for months to take a long rest. Now he had no excuse for ignoring the advice. After the first shock of his defeat wore off, he said he was happy to be painting again, and to read novels—a form of literature he had always said he had no time for. He and Clemmie played his favorite card game, bezique. He dozed in the sun.

For a while he showed little interest in politics. Other members of his party, who had lived so long under his domination, seemed relieved to be free of it. They congratulated him when he roused himself to start a history of the war, which would eventually fill six large volumes. They said it would keep him busy. Some even said it would permit him to live in the past, where he belonged.

Again, as in his earlier war history, he used many of the memos, letters, and directives he had issued while the fighting was going on. He told his readers that although these papers might show he had made a few mistakes, he believed they would prove he had almost always been right. At the beginning of each volume he

Churchill relaxes by painting a landscape.

repeated what he called the "Moral of the Work." He said it summed up his philosophy:

> In War: Resolution
> In Defeat: Defiance
> In Victory: Magnanimity
> In Peace: Good Will

Before the final volume was published, he would be awarded the Nobel Prize for Literature.

Eight months after leaving office he and Clemmie went to the United States where he was to receive an honorary degree from Westminster College. Other far better-known institutions had already bestowed degrees on this man who had never attended a university and who had failed so many examinations in his school days. He was willing to travel so far to accept this degree because he was ready to make a statement to the world.

Westminster College is in Fulton, Missouri. President Truman, a Missouri native, introduced Churchill who, in his acceptance speech, declared that an "iron curtain" had descended across Europe. Behind it, he said, was the Soviet Union and the "Soviet sphere." To prevent the enlargement of that sphere he called for a united Western Europe and an Anglo-American alliance, strong enough to meet any threat from the Soviet Union.

His words shocked many old admirers who said Churchill was proving to be, after all, the warmonger he had often been called, the adventurer seeking one more battlefield. Churchill's reply was that he abhorred war; that the existence of the atomic bomb made the possibility of a third world war utterly unthinkable; and that he was suggesting the only means by which it could be avoided: the same kind of unity against possible aggression which he insisted could have prevented both world wars if nations had only been wise enough to adopt it. Before those earlier wars he had preached unity chiefly with other European countries; now he regarded the United States, newly risen to world power, as England's most valuable ally.

From then on he appeared more often in Parliament,

to declare the Labor party's policy weak and fumbling, its domestic programs socialistic and therefore dangerous. The party had nationalized, or brought under public ownership, the Bank of England. It planned to nationalize certain industries too, so that their profits would belong to the people. It talked of setting up a national health scheme to provide free medical service for all.

"A short time ago I was ready to retire and die gracefully," he told his doctor. Now he was ready to start fighting the Labor party and put it out of office. "I'm in pretty good fettle," he insisted, and said he owed his healthy condition to "the Jerome blood."

The Labor party was struggling desperately with an economy still exhausted by war. New troubles beset the nation constantly. She could afford so little imported wheat that bread had to be rationed. Right after the coal industry was nationalized, bad weather kept coal from reaching the cities and that too had to be restricted. People grumbled, in spite of their approval of the new health program and other Labor party reforms.

Many people also felt angry and humiliated, as Churchill himself did, at the way the once-vast British Empire was shrinking: India had won independence; the Republic of Ireland cut all ties with Britain; Egypt was threatening to end British authority in the Sudan. Englishmen were muttering that Churchill would never

A victorious Churchill greets the crowds after he becomes prime minister for the second time in 1951. Clemmie can be seen behind the closed window.

have allowed such things to happen, if he had remained in power.

In the meantime the government was taking some of the steps in foreign relations that Churchill had been urging. Britain signed treaties with several European nations and became a member of NATO, the North Atlantic Treaty Organization. As fear of communism grew throughout the Western world, British soldiers joined the United Nations force fighting North Korean and Chinese Communist forces in South Korea.

Although Churchill approved such moves, he did not approve of those men—most of them Americans—who had begun to urge that the West enter upon a full-scale war with the Soviet Union immediately, while the West was still superior to the Communists in atomic weapons. Churchill insisted that when he talked of the need to be prepared for war, he was in reality talking of the only real road to peace.

In 1949 Churchill had suffered a slight stroke. He ignored that danger sign and campaigned strenuously before the 1950 election. The Labor party won, but by such a small majority that it was forced to call another election the next year. That time the Conservatives were victorious and Churchill, as their leader, became prime minister for a second time. He was within a month of his seventy-seventh birthday.

He moved back to 10 Downing Street a weary and

visibly aging man. He could still grin triumphantly, however, at the crowd waiting for him there, and raise his hand in the old V-for-victory sign.

"I believe I may be able to make an important contribution to the prevention of a third world war," he said. "It is the last prize I seek."

He showed his old vigor when he crossed the Atlantic shortly afterward to further cement England's partnership with the United States—a partnership he hoped to direct toward peaceful coexistence with the Soviet Union. He seemed less vigorous when he returned home to the daily "box" that demanded his attention each morning. Economics had never really interested him, and most of the daily problems he now faced were economic. The work made him restless and impatient. The strain brought on another stroke.

When he recovered, he began to talk of resigning in favor of Anthony Eden, his minister of foreign affairs. Many felt he would be wise to do so. No one had the courage to tell him they felt the time had come for him to give up his role of party leader and prime minister. And Churchill himself changed his mind about resigning every time he seemed to have made the decision.

His old friend King George VI died, and Churchill decided to remain in office until after the ceremonial crowning of the new young Queen Elizabeth, set for June 1953.

Copyright Toni Frissell, 1959

Churchill, his son, and grandson pose in lavish
dress for the coronation of Elizabeth II.

The queen was crowned and still Churchill stayed stubbornly on, although now the opposition press was demanding his resignation.

"I can do something with the Russians which no one else can do," he said. "That is the only reason why I am clinging to office."

In June 1954 he was in Washington once more, conferring with his old friend Eisenhower, now president of the United States. He was unable to win American agreement to his own conviction that Communist China be brought into the United Nations in order to further the peaceful settlement of disputes between that country and the Western world. He did come away from the meeting, however, feeling that he had won an ally for his own stand about the Soviet Union.

Eisenhower, he told a friend with obvious relief, "has made up his mind that Communism is not something which we must at all costs wipe out, but rather something we have got to learn to live with, and alongside…"

In October he attended the Conservative party conference. At the party's conference the previous year many men had been sure they were hearing him speak for the last time. Now they found him as energetic as he had been in the war years. He beamed from the platform, aware that they expected him to talk of resigning but that they seemed happy enough when he refused to mention it. The press reported that the members were content "that he should go in his own time and how he pleases."

In November the whole nation celebrated Churchill's eightieth birthday. He was Sir Winston Churchill now, having accepted from the young queen the knighthood he had earlier been offered and had refused. A stream of birthday gifts arrived at 10 Downing Street from all over the world. Members of the House of Commons presented him with a portrait of himself.

After making it clear to a packed House that he didn't much like the portrait, which he thought made him look old and angry, Churchill went on with a modesty which surprised many who knew him. He said he was often given credit for inspiring the nation during the grim days when England stood alone against her enemies.

"It was the nation and the race dwelling round the globe that had the lion's heart," he said. "I had the luck to be called upon to give the roar."

The affection of all men seemed to be his that day. It belonged to him still three months later when he came to the House to make his farewell speech as prime minister. He was resigning at last.

He and Clemmie moved out of 10 Downing Street on April 6, 1955. They returned to Chartwell Manor with its goldfish pond, where Churchill daily fed the fish, and with its stables, where he bred race horses with the help of one of his sons-in-law. Here at Chartwell he painted too and soon began to write one more large work, *A History of the English-Speaking People.*

He was still a member of Parliament, although he seldom attended its sessions now. He was eighty-seven when he entered the House of Commons for the last time and found himself unable to say more than the few simple words, "I am grateful to you all."

Each of his birthdays now was a national event, celebrated far beyond England's borders. Soon after his eighty-eighth birthday, the Congress of the United States declared him an honorary citizen—a tribute paid to only one other man, the Marquis de Lafayette.

"By adding his name to our rolls, we mean to honor him—but his acceptance honors us far more," President John F. Kennedy said. "For no statement or proclamation can enrich his name now—the name Sir Winston Churchill is already legend."

His death came quietly on January 24, 1965, on the seventieth anniversary of the day his father had died. His father had been forty-six. Churchill had lived two months past his ninetieth birthday.

By Queen Elizabeth's decree his body lay in state in Westminster Hall, where the bodies of England's monarchs and her greatest heroes had lain. Hour after hour, for three days and nights, men, women, and children waited in the bitter winter cold to file past his flag-draped coffin. Then the coffin was borne in a solemn state procession to St. Paul's Cathedral. Among the mourners were many heads of state—sixteen prime ministers, four kings, and two queens. England's Elizabeth broke royal tradition to attend the funeral of this commoner who had been the devoted subject of six English sovereigns.

He was buried at his own request beside his parents in the little country churchyard near Blenheim Palace. Today his simple grave and the great stone palace are places of pilgrimage for thousands. To many Blenheim is now better known as Churchill's birthplace than as the monument erected to his lifelong hero, the first duke of Marlborough.

Harold Macmillan, one of Sir Winston's oldest friends and political allies, said of him in the House of Commons, "The oldest among us can recall nothing to compare with him, and the younger ones among us, however long we live, will never see the like again."

Sir Winston Churchill's title for the final volume of his World War II history had expressed his feeling that "the overwhelming victory of the Grand Alliance has failed so far to bring general peace to our anxious world." He had called it *Triumph and Tragedy*. He had known both experiences in his own life. Only history itself will be able to judge which, in his long career, were the real tragedies, and which were the greatest triumphs; but it is already possible to say that his place in history is secure for all time.

Chronological List of Events
in Winston Churchill's Life

1874   Winston Leonard Spencer-Churchill is born at Blenheim Palace on November 30 to Lord Randolph Spencer-Churchill and his wife, the former Jennie Jerome of New York. Winston is educated at Harrow and the Royal Military College at Sandhurst.

1895   Churchill enters the army as a lieutenant with the Fourth Hussars. While on leave, he goes to Cuba as a newspaperman to report on the Spanish army campaign against the Cuban rebels.

1898   With the Twenty-first Lancers in Egypt, Churchill fights Dervish tribesmen in the battle for Omdurman.

1899   Churchill loses his first election for the House of Commons. Later that year, he goes to Africa to report on the Boer War for the London *Morning Post*. In November, he is captured by the Boers and imprisoned in Pretoria. He soon manages to escape.

1900   In October, Churchill is elected to the House of Commons as a Conservative, or Tory, member from Oldham.

1906   Churchill is appointed under secretary of state for the colonies, a position he holds until 1908.

1908   The marriage of Winston Churchill and Clementine Ogilvy Hozier takes place. The same year, he assumes the position of president of the board of trade.

1910   Churchill serves his country as home secretary.

1911   Churchill is appointed first lord of the admiralty. He greatly increases Britain's naval strength and creates the navy's first air service, preparing the nation for World War I.

1915   Following the defeat of British naval forces at Gallipoli in World War I, Churchill loses his cabinet post as first lord of the admiralty. He assumes command of the Sixth Royal Scots Fusiliers in France.

1916   Churchill resumes his seat in the House of Commons.

1917   Churchill becomes minister of munitions in the cabinet formed by Liberal Prime Minister Lloyd George.

1922   The Churchills purchase Chartwell Manor, a home where the family retreats for relaxation and country living.

1924 Churchill becomes chancellor of the exchequer (in a Tory government). This position was once held by his father.

1939 When war is declared on Germany on September 3, Churchill is again called upon to serve as first lord of the admiralty.

1940 On April 4, Churchill is appointed minister of defense, and on May 10, he succeeds Neville Chamberlain as prime minister. With brilliance and enormous confidence, he leads his people through World War II, inspiring them with his frequent speeches and radio messages.

1945 Churchill and his Conservative party lose the elections in July to the Labor party.

1951 In October Churchill is again elected prime minister.

1953 Churchill is made Knight of the Garter in April by Queen Elizabeth II. He is now known as Sir Winston Churchill. In October he is awarded the Nobel Prize for Literature for his six-volume history of World War II.

1963 Churchill is made an honorary citizen of the United States.

1965 Sir Winston Churchill, age 90, dies on January 24.

Index

52, 57, 58, 59, 60, 78, 80, 81,
83, 84, 89, 90, 94, 95, 99, 100,
102, 105, 108, 109, 119, 120,
123, 124, 130, 134, 135, 139,
148, 149, 154, 155, 158, 162,
165, 166
English Channel, 100, 123, 129
Estcourt, Natal, 61, 63
Everest, Elizabeth Anne (nurse), 18,
109, 115

F

Fourth Hussars, 31, 32, 39, 40, 41,
42, 43–44, 53, 57
France, 26, 95, 99, 100, 105, 110, 119,
120, 122, 123, 124, 125, 147,
148, 149

G

Gallipoli Peninsula, 103, 107
Gandhi, Mohandas, 141
George V, King, 93
George VI, King, 120–121, 128, 147,
153 (pic), 162
Germany, 95, 99, 100, 117, 119, 120,
129, 132, 134, 145, 149, 152,
154
Gibbon, Edward, 42

H

Haldane, Aylmer, 62–64, 67, 70, 71,
80
Harrow, 26, 29
Hitler, Adolph, 117, 119, 120, 124,
129, 131, 132, 134, 135, 143,
150, 151
House of Commons, 15, 17, 24, 25,
42, 53, 58, 81, 82, 83, 84, 85,
86, 87, 88, 92, 93, 94, 97, 107,
109, 112, 117, 122, 132, 133
(pic), 165, 166, 167
House of Lords, 83, 92, 93
Howard, John, 75–76
Hozier, Clementine. *See* Churchill,
Clementine

I

India, 32, 33, 38, 39, 40, 43, 53, 57,
62, 114, 140, 141, 159
Iran, 97, 146
Ireland, 18, 87, 94, 159
Italy, 145

J

Japan, 137, 152, 153, 155
Jerome, Clara, 14
Jerome, Jennie. *See* Churchill, Jennie
Jerome, Leonard, 14–15, 17, 33, 35

K

Kaffirs, 73, 76
Kennedy, John F., 166
Kent, 109
Khartoum, Africa, 49
Kitchener, Horatio H. (Lord), 102,
103
Komati Poort, South Africa, 76

L

Labor party, 84, 91, 93, 111, 152, 154,
159, 161
Ladysmith, Natal, 61, 79
Lafayette, Marquis de, 166
League of Nations, 108, 118
Lend-Lease plan, 131
Lenin, Vladimir I., 132
Liberal party, 15, 24, 58, 82, 84, 87,
88, 89, 92, 93, 94, 105, 107,
111, 112
Liverpool, 130
Lloyd George, David (prime minis-
ter), 91, 107, 108 -
London, 9, 10, 12, 17, 21, 34, 42, 48,
56, 78, 90, 101, 102, 103, 109,
114, 126, 128, 130, 131, 132,
147, 148, 149
Lord Randolph Churchill, 88
Lourenço Marques, 76, 77
Luxembourg, 120

M

Macaulay, Thomas, 42
Macmillan, Harold (prime minister), 167
Mafeking, Cape Colony, 61
Malta, 131
Manchester, 88
Marlborough, duchess of, 18, 53
Marlborough, first duke of, 13, 17, 25, 29, 33, 116, 167
Marlborough, ninth duke of (Sunny), 83, 84
Marlborough, seventh duke of, 13, 14, 15, 17, 18, 20, 26, 33, 35
Morning Post, 55, 60, 61, 62, 74, 78
Moscow, 142
Mussolini, Benito, 117, 119, 145
My Early Life, 115, 116

N

Natal, 60, 61
Nazi forces, 119, 124, 125, 134, 142
Netherlands, 120, 123
Newfoundland, 134
New York, 14, 34
Nile River, 49
Nobel Prize for Literature, 157
North Africa, 117, 128, 131, 141, 142, 143
North Atlantic Treaty Organization (NATO), 161
North Korea, 161
Norway, 120

O

Oldham, 57, 58, 59, 75, 81, 82
Omdurman, battle of, 49, 50 (pic), 51, 52
Orange Free State, 60

P

Pacific Ocean, 137, 140, 153
Palestine, 109
Paris, 101, 123, 124, 149
Parliament, 7, 15, 42, 43, 54, 57, 59, 81, 83, 84, 85, 87, 89, 92, 93, 94, 103, 111, 115, 122, 142, 154, 158, 166
Pathan tribesmen, 43–46
Pearl Harbor, 137
Persia. *See* Iran
Pioneer, 43
Poland, 119
Portuguese East Africa, 72, 76
Potsdam Conference, 152–153
Pretoria, 72, 74, 78, 79
Prince of Wales (later King Edward VII), 17, 48
Prince of Wales, 134

R

Reynaud, Paul, 122, 123
Rommel, Erwin, 131
Roosevelt, Eleanor (Mrs. Franklin D. Roosevelt), 145
Roosevelt, Elliott, 145
Roosevelt, Franklin D., 130, 131, 134–135, 137, 138, 141, 142, 143, 145, 146, 150 (pic), 151, 152, 154
Royal Air Force, 125
Royal Military College, 7–9, 26, 29, 31, 42, 115
Royal Navy Air Service, 100
Russia, 99, 108, 132, 134, 135, 142, 150, 151. *See also* Soviet Union

S

St. George's School, 21, 23
St. Paul's Cathedral, 167
Salisbury, Robert Arthur Talbot Gascoyne-Cecil, Lord (prime minister), 48
Sandhurst. *See* Royal Military College
Savrola, 53, 80
Scotland, 84
Scots fusiliers, 106–107
Sikhs, 44
South Africa, 34, 60
South Korea, 161
Southampton, 130